Andrews University

Seventh-day Adventist Theological Seminary

A STRATEGY FOR DEVELOPING OUTREACH-ORIENTED
SMALL GROUPS FOR MILLENNIAL STUDENTS AT
GEORGIA-CUMBERLAND ACADEMY CHURCH

A Project Document

Presented in Partial Fulfillment

of the Requirements for the Degree

Doctor of Ministry

by

Greg Hudson

August 2017

World rights reserved. This book or any portion thereof may not be copied or reproduced in any form or manner whatever, except as provided by law, without the written permission of the publisher, except by a reviewer who may quote brief passages in a review.

The author assumes full responsibility for the accuracy of all facts and quotations as cited in this book. The opinions expressed in this book are the author's personal views and interpretations, and do not necessarily reflect those of the publisher.

This book is provided with the understanding that the publisher is not engaged in giving spiritual, legal, medical, or other professional advice. If authoritative advice is needed, the reader should seek the counsel of a competent professional.

_____

Copyright©2017 Gregory P. Hudson
Copyright©2017 TEACHServices, Inc.
ISBN-13: 978-1-4796-0855-3 (Paperback)
Library of Congress Control Number: 2017916158

To my Wife, Joely,
and Peyton, Brandon, and Jordan

You have put up with my late nights,
many hours of reading,
and constant time on the computer.
Thanks and much love to you all!

TABLE OF CONTENTS

LIST OF TABLES viii

LIST OF FIGURES viii

ACKNOWLEDGMENTS ix

Chapter
1. INTRODUCTION 1

       Personal Ministry Context. 2
       Purpose 2
       Statement of the Problem 3
       Justification for the Project 5
       Expectations of the Project 6
       Delimitations 7
       Limitations 7
       Definition of Terms. 8
       Description of Methodology 9
       Summary 10

2. A THEOLOGICAL REFLECTION ON YOUTH INVOLVEMENT IN SMALL GROUPS FOR TRANSFORMATIONAL COMMUNITY EVANGELISM 12

       Participants in Evangelism 13
           Defining Evangelism 13
           Called to Evangelism 15
           Biblical Examples 16
       Gathering for Evangelism 18
           Old Testament 18
           Jesus in the Gospels 19
           The Church in Acts 20
           House Churches 22
           "One Another" Passages 22
           Outreach in Small Groups 23
           Small Group Summary 23
       Models of Evangelism 24
           Transformational Community Evangelism 25

    Ultimate Source of Help—God 25
    Incarnational Example of Help—Jesus. 26
    Ongoing Community of Help—God's People 27
    Summary. 28
   Proclamational Evangelism 29
    The Ministry of Jesus 29
    The Apostles 29
   Complimentary Ministry 31
   Summary 31
  Summary of Theological Reflection 32

3. LITERATURE REVIEW OF MILLENNIAL INVOLVEMENT IN
  TRANSFORMATIONAL EVANGELISM. 34

  Studies on the Millennial Generation 35
   General Characteristics of the Millennial Generation 35
   Spiritual Characteristics of the Millennial Generation. 37
    Millennials and the Church. 37
    Moralistic Therapeutic Deism. 38
    Spiritual, But Not Religious 39
   Implications 40
  Types of Community Outreach Philosophies 40
   Missional 40
   Development of Outreach Ideas. 42
    Organic Church. 42
    Simple Discipleship 42
    Externally Focused Church. 43
    Graceful Evangelism. 43
    Transformational Church 44
   Implications 44
  Studies in Community Development 44
   Discovering Community Needs. 44
   Community Transformation. 46
   Implications 48
  Training Millennials for Transformational Outreach 48
   Why Train Millennials. 49
    Spiritual Growth 49
    Millennial Desire to Make a Difference 51
   How to Train Millennials for Transformational Outreach. 52
    Small Groups 52
    Mentoring 55
    Active Learning and Reflection 56
   Implications 57
   Brief Survey of Writings of Ellen White 57

  Summary and Implications of Literary Findings 59

4. A METHODOLGY AND IMPLEMENTATION OF OUTREACH-
   ORIENTED SMALL GROUPS 62

   Introduction 62
   The Setting for Ministry 64
   From Captured Hearts to Developed Disciples 66
   Know, Grow, Go 69
   The Basic7 Plan 70
   Exploring a Process for Outreach-Oriented Small Groups 72
      Small Groups for Fellowship and Training 72
      Assessing Community Needs 73
      Service-Oriented Outreach 73
   Exploring Successful Small Group Strategies 74
      Church 1: Richardson, Texas, Seventh-day Adventist Church,
         Dan Serns, Senior Pastor 74
      Church 2: Pioneer Memorial Church, Berrien Springs, Michigan,
         Rodlie Ortiz, Pastor for Outreach/Evangelism 75
      Activate, by Nelson Searcy 76
   Implementation of a Strategy for Outreach-Oriented Small Groups .. 77
      Small Group Foundation 77
      Evaluating Community Needs 78
      Project Groups 79
         Group Leader Training Series 79
         Reach the World Small Group Curriculum 81
   Conclusion and Implications 82

5. OUTCOMES AND EVALUATIONS 84

   Introduction 84
   Summary of Project 85
   GROWgroups in Action 87
      Year 1 87
      Year 2 88
   The Small Group Process 89
   Analysis of Surveys 92
      Changes in Promotion 93
      Benefits of Personal/Community Spirituality 94
      Benefits in Community/Social Aspects 95
      Benefits in Service/Outreach Attitude 96
   Potential Improvements 96
   Recommendations for Further Study 97
      Different Forms of Small Groups 98
      Impact of Cross-Generational Groups 99
      Different Methods of Outreach 99
      Changes in Future Generations 100
   Recommendations for Greater Impact 101

      Ongoing Impact of GROWgroups 102
      Personal Growth 103
      Conclusion. 105

Appendix
    A. SMALL GROUP STRATEGY INTERVIEWS. 107
    B. QUESTIONNAIRES 111
    C. COMMUNITY LEADER INTERVIEWS. 115
    D. *REACH THE WORLD* LESSONS 119
    E. SURVEY RAW DATA RESULTS 125

REFERENCE LIST 126

VITA. 134

LIST OF TABLES

1. Dates, Topics, and Information for Video Sessions 80
2. Topics and Theme of Each Lesson of *Reach the World* Curriculum 82
3. Survey Raw Data Results- Averages of Answers from Year 1 and Year 2 95

LIST OF FIGURES

1. The Membership and Baptisms of the GCA Church (2003-2016) 66
2. Percentage of GROWgroup Participation Among Students, 2014-2016 94

ACKNOWLEGEMENTS

First, I thank God and give praise to Him for the gift of life eternal. It is amazing that God takes a sinner like me and gives me the opportunity to tell others about the free gift of amazing grace.

I thank Dr. Russell Burrill, my project adviser, for his support and guidance through this process. He has been an inspiration and friend from teaching seminary classes in evangelism, to my time working at NADEI, to his many inspiring books.

I thank others who have inspired me in the field of evangelism: Dr. Ron Clouzet for teaching evangelism classes at Southern Adventist University, and starting off this DMIN cohort; Dr. Ed Schmidt for being a personal evangelism guru and my second reader for this project; the late Elder Ron Halverson Sr., for helping to instill a passion to reach others through a short time at an Evangelistic Field School; Elder Jim Gilley, my first conference president, for believing in a young pastor.

I thank those that have inspired me in the field of Youth Ministry: John Swafford, Don Keele Jr., and Rob Lang, as well as my Pathfinder leaders through the years. You have shown me how to love young people and introduce them to Jesus.

I thank the Georgia-Cumberland Academy Church, and the students and staff at Georgia-Cumberland Academy, for eager participation and ongoing support through many years of laughter and ministering together.

CHAPTER 1

INTRODUCTION

From the time I first felt called to serve God as a pastor, I have had two ministry passions: youth ministry and evangelism. First, by ministering to the youth in the church and helping them to experience the grace of God, I anticipate they will recognize the call of God in their lives for service to the church and community. Second, I desire to remind church members, young and old, that the Great Commission of Matthew 28 challenges all believers to "Go and make disciples."

I have tried to make these two passions the pillars of my ministry. I have ministered to young people through Pathfinders, youth rallies, chaplaincy, church schools, and building friendships. Evangelism has been done through a variety of means including personal Bible studies, radio ministry shows, service projects, and public evangelistic meetings in the local church and across the globe.

This project is an attempt to meld these two passions into one coherent strategy to disciple young people and to engage them in outreach ministry. I hope to show that youth are not simply to be the targets of evangelism, but they can be trained and equipped to be workers for evangelism and outreach. I believe that small groups are an ideal way to minister to young people while training and inspiring them to work for God and to share their faith.

Personal Ministry Context

I currently serve as the senior pastor of the Georgia-Cumberland Academy Seventh-day Adventist Church on the campus of Georgia-Cumberland Academy (GCA). This church of about 280 members has a primary ministry focus to the 250 academy students that attend this boarding high school. The GCA Church is in Calhoun, Georgia, and is part of the Georgia-Cumberland Conference of Seventh-day Adventists. Pastoring in this context allows the opportunity to serve three constituencies: community church members, school staff, and students. The challenge is to help these three distinct groups to worship together, and to grow in their spiritual walk and their service to God.

From 2002-2014, I served as the associate pastor of the GCA Church and campus chaplain for GCA. In 2014, I transitioned to the role of senior pastor. Prior to 2002, I had served as a local church pastor in several districts in Arkansas, and also as a registered nurse.

Purpose

The purpose of this project is to develop, implement, and evaluate a church-wide, outreach-oriented small group strategy at the GCA Church to engage GCA students in community-based service opportunities. A foundation for church-wide groups is to be developed, community needs are to be assessed, and outreach ideas developed to witness to the community.

The premise of this research is to show that as Millennial students are engaged in an active small-group community, they would be inspired and equipped to engage in outreach projects. As they participate in the biblical model of connecting with Jesus and with each other, they would be motivated to fulfill the Gospel Commission by taking part in evangelistic opportunities to meet the felt needs of those around them. It is believed that as young people engage in this type of outreach, it would strengthen and enhance their connection to God and to the church.

Statement of the Problem

Studies show that up to 60% of youth and young adults in America are leaving the church (Smith & Snell, 2009; Kinnaman & Hawkins, 2011; Powell, Mulder, & Griffin, 2016). The church cannot sustain this continued loss of membership, especially from the ranks of young people. A recent study by Barna Group (2013b) for the North American Division of Seventh-day Adventists (SDA) reveals very similar statistics in the Adventist Church. This is already impacting the mission and ministry of the church and creating a gap in church membership.

This gap is generating what is referred to by some as "the graying of Adventism," indicating that church membership is disproportionally skewed toward older members. More recent statistics reported by the Office of Archives, Statistics, and Research of the General Conference of Seventh-day Adventists indicate that in North America the average age of the members of the Adventist Church is 51, much higher than the world-wide average of 32 (Trim, 2016). In fact, only 4.55% of Adventists in North America are under the age of 25. Clearly, the Adventist Church faces the problem of reaching and retaining young people as an active part of the church family. This problem is similar to what other denominations face as well.

Powell and Clark (2011) indicate that a key factor that helps to encourage young people to remain in church is their connection and participation in the ministries of the church. In fact, young people appreciate the opportunity to meet the needs of others

(Stetzer, Stanley, & Hayes, 2009, p. 111). These findings agree that active engagement in the life and outreach of the church is instrumental in building the spiritual commitment of young people that will contribute to ongoing membership and participation within the church.

This idea of engaging youth in ministry has long been part of the strategy of the Adventist Church, even if it is not always practiced as it should be. Regarding outreach ministry, Ellen White, one of the founders of the Seventh-day Adventist Church, remarks, "There is no line of work in which it is possible for the youth to receive greater benefit," and calls for "an army of youth, rightly trained" to take the message of the gospel to the world (White, 1903, p. 271). White also maintained that "those who are most actively employed in doing with interested fidelity their work to win souls to Jesus Christ, are the best developed in spirituality and devotion" (1946, p. 356). This clearly indicates that ministry activity positively affects spiritual growth and will help solidify an individual's walk with God.

Many students at GCA are involved in ministry tasks within the church, but far fewer are voluntarily involved in ongoing outreach and evangelistic activities. While about 33% of students are active in leadership in church activities and 30% are involved in short-term mission trips, less than 10% are engaged in regular, ongoing evangelistic and outreach events. GCA is a boarding school with almost 80% of the students having homes in other locations. Since most students live in other places, they therefore have limited opportunity to develop connections with the local community, both at home and at school. The result is that students are graduating without needed skills to spiritually interact with their community and to share their faith in Jesus in meaningful ways.

Contributing factors to this challenge are a lack of opportunity to build meaningful relationships in the local community, a lack of outreach training for students, and a lack of personal motivation to witness.

Justification for the Project

Even though the Adventist Church is growing at a faster rate than other denominations in the United States, it still is not gaining much ground against the growth rate of the country as a whole. The growth rate of Adventist Church has slowed from its earlier history, while the population of the United States continues to grow rapidly. The Adventist Church is barely keeping up, and something needs to change (Beckworth & Kidder, 2010). Prayer and an outpouring of the Holy Spirit are obviously the most important needs for mission, but without a change in mission participation among members of the church, it seems impossible to successfully reach the country and the world with the message of Jesus. Students need to be equipped and inspired to make fulfilling the Gospel Commission an active part of their daily life. As individuals make this a priority in life from a young age, it can potentially remain a part of their lifestyle and could be a contributing factor to their remaining an active Christian.

Following the biblical paradigm of Acts 2:42, this project seeks to encourage students to participate in outreach-oriented small groups. As students, together with church members, form community in small groups and grow in their personal spiritual walk, they will be inspired and equipped to utilize their gifts in serving the people around them.

This project will be an integral part in developing an ongoing student discipleship strategy, encouraging young people to progress in three ways: (a) to *know*, (b) to *grow*, and (c) to *go*. As students participate in personal Bible study and small groups they will *know* God in a more personal and developed manner. Students will *grow* in their spiritual gifts, as well as in their Christian life and walk, as they are trained and equipped to be involved in the ministries of the church. Finally, students should respond to the Gospel Commission to *go* and share the message of Jesus through personal, public, and global outreach. Outreach-oriented small groups will assist students to engage in transformational community evangelism while moving through the facets of this discipleship strategy. Students may enter this three-fold process with any of the steps and grow through the process in any order.

This project examines various models of outreach-oriented small groups, develops a church-wide discipleship strategy with a small group foundation, encourages groups to engage in gospel outreach to help transform communities by exploring and meeting real and felt needs, examines the results of this strategy, and finally, explores the implications of a small group strategy for potential use in other contexts.

Expectations of the Project

This project has aided one church in the development of a small group strategy. The process of implementing this church-wide program has been a reminder of the importance of small groups to fostering personal spiritual growth and community among members and students. This program has resulted in an academy-focused church developing an ongoing small group program, fostering cross-generational community between students and church members, training new leaders, as well as encouraging and equipping young people to be more engaged in outreach.

This project could also serve as a model for other Seventh-day Adventist churches to adapt or build upon, especially churches with a high ratio of youth to church members.

It is the intent of this project to contribute to the development of a model for inspiring, training, and equipping Seventh-day Adventist young people to be involved in outreach to their community through small groups in a local church setting.

Delimitations

This project was instituted with the belief that participation in outreach-oriented small groups will help young people to be more active in evangelism and outreach in the community. With potentially improved personal spiritual lives and more people inspired to serve the community, it is thought that this will result in the local church membership growing larger through active outreach resulting in baptisms, but that is beyond the scope of this study.

This project was done in the context of the GCA Church, but the primary focus of the study was on the students at GCA. While several adult church members participated in various aspects of this project, the research was centered on the response of the students.

Limitations

This project was limited in several areas, including time and scope. While the project involved two academic years at GCA, it is understood that each school, and even each school year, includes different students and contexts, and therefore may yield differing results, but it is believed that the findings of this study would be transferable to different Seventh-day Adventist churches and schools in the North American Division.

The participants in this study were GCA students who voluntarily took part in small groups, training, and surveys. The project assumes that this group is fairly representative of the entire student body, as well as students in general, but it is recognized that students who voluntarily participate in small groups may begin the process at a different spiritual level than others.

Students were invited to return surveys at the beginning and end of each school year, giving quantitative data to be used for analysis (see Appendix B). This data is used to examine the perceived benefit of the small group strategy is various areas of the students' lives.

Definition of Terms

There are several terms that are used throughout this project that deserve defining for the sake of clarity. The word *community* is used in two ways in this project. First, the idea of *community* is a bond of friendship and fellowship between church members and members of a small group. A key element in the life of the church is "authentic community—the kind of meaningful relationships that are best characterized by oneness with Him and with one another" (Stanley & Willits, 2004, p. 40). Second, the location of *community* is the neighborhood, town, and surrounding regions, where students and church members are encouraged to look for ways to minister and share their faith (see Sahlin, 2004, p. ii). The context should make clear which type of *community* is being referenced.

The initials *GCA* refers to Georgia-Cumberland Academy, a Seventh-day Adventist secondary boarding school in Calhoun, Georgia, serving about 250 students in grades 9-12. The phrase *GCA Church* refers to the congregation that meets on the campus of GCA. This local congregation contains about 280 members made up of local community members and GCA staff, and during the academic year it serves as the church home for the students of GCA.

Students refer to the high school students of GCA. These students are in grades 9-12, and during the school year take an active part in many of the ministries of the GCA Church.

The phrase *outreach-oriented small groups* refers to gatherings of individuals for an intentional purpose of growing in fellowship with each other, as well as devoting some time to active involvement in outreach (Searcy, 2008).

Transformational Community Evangelism refers to the recognition of various types of needs in a local community, and working to assist in meeting those needs.

Description of Methodology

The primary goal of this project was to examine a biblical and theological perspective of outreach-oriented small groups, to implement a church-wide small group initiative, and to analyze the mission-impact on students at GCA.

Many different steps were involved in this process. First, theological guidance was gleaned from scripture, focusing on key elements of biblical small groups in the ministry of Jesus and the disciples. The correlation of transformational and proclamational evangelism was also examined. Second, there was a review of recent, pertinent literature focusing on the Millennial generation, forms of outreach-oriented small groups, community-based outreach, and suggested training methodologies. Third, based on these studies, as well as interviews with pastors leading successful outreach-oriented small group ministries, a strategy for implementing outreach-oriented small groups in the local church was developed utilizing a three-fold plan of small group formation, evaluating community needs, and developing group-based evangelism projects. Finally, groups, outreach techniques, and surveys were analyzed to discover positive aspects of the implementation, and to suggest changes for the future.

Outreach-oriented small groups, referred to as GROWgroups, were developed church-wide over the course of two academic years. Group leaders were recruited and trained, and each semester a new set of affinity-based groups was organized and formed. Students were given the opportunity to return surveys at the beginning and end of each year (see Appendix B). These surveys were analyzed to determine students' perceptions of the value of GROWgroup participation in various areas of their life, including evangelism, social, and spiritual.

Summary

The present study is comprised of five chapters. Chapter 1 is a brief introduction with an outline of the problem studied by this project, a statement of the task, justification for the project, brief description of the methodology followed, and previews of the other chapters. Chapter 2 is a discussion of the biblical and theological foundation for small groups as a means of inspiration and training for outreach. Chapter 3 examines relevant literature regarding the characteristics of the Millennial generation, outreach-oriented small groups, community outreach, and evangelistic training. Chapter 4 describes the ministry context and outlines the development of a church-wide small group strategy and the implementation at the GCA Church. Chapter 5 analyzes outcomes of the project and offers suggestions for further exploration.

The purpose of this project was to develop a strategy for implementing outreach-oriented small groups for young people to engage them in community-based service opportunities. The following chapters document this process.

CHAPTER 2

A THEOLOGICAL REFLECTION ON YOUTH INVOLVEMENT
IN SMALL GROUPS FOR TRANSFORMATIONAL
COMMUNITY EVANGELISM

The purpose of this chapter is to develop a theology of small groups and transformational community evangelism with an emphasis on youth involvement. Much of today's literature regarding youth ministry places an emphasis on "reaching the youth" (DeVries, 2008). While it is of vital importance for young people to make decisions for Christ during their teen years (Barna Group, 2004), statistics still show that 60% of young adults are leaving the church (Kinnaman & Hawkins, 2011).

This study desires to see beyond youth and young adults as being merely the targets of evangelism, and to attempt to engage Millennials as active participants in evangelizing others, both young and old. These participants in outreach should include all followers of Jesus, regardless of age, as the Bible clearly indicates with the idea of the "priesthood of all believers" (1 Pet 2:9).

This chapter will examine the Old and New Testament for principles regarding young people being involved in transformational community outreach. Because of the limitations of time and space this research will not be exhaustive, but will be limited in scope to several key elements: participants in evangelism, the gathering for evangelism, and two models of evangelism. More specifically, this chapter will examine the biblical precedence of young people being involved in spreading the message of God, small groups as a place of training and fellowship for the purpose of evangelism, and will compare two different models of evangelism, the complimentary methods of transformational and proclamational evangelism. The chapter will end with a brief selection of statements on these same topics from the writings of Ellen White, one of the co-founders of the Seventh-day Adventist Church.

Participants in Evangelism

A theology of youth involvement in evangelism begins with a definition of this term and then turns to an exploration of the comprehensive call to participate in God's mission.

Defining Evangelism

"Evangelism" is derived from the Greek word εὐαγγέλιον, which simply means "good news" or "gospel" (Nichol, 1953, p. 471). This refers to the message of Jesus Christ that is to be proclaimed to the world. Kidder (2011) notes that the word "evangelism" does not appear in the New King James Version, while the word "evangelist" occurs only three times (Acts 21:8; Eph 4:11; 2 Tim 4:5), each time referring to the title or role of a person who is sharing this good news (p. 23).

Evangelism is more than just communicating a message. A true definition of "evangelism" involves a life-changing experience and a call to ministry. Leonard (2008) surmises that evangelism, an idea so central to the purpose of the Christian church, is difficult to adequately define. He uses this three-fold explanation: "Christian evangelism is the good news that Jesus Christ is the way to God. It is the proclamation of the story of

Jesus and the call to follow him. Evangelism also involves the living out of that good news in the world" (p. 102).

Bosch (2008) states that evangelism is

> that dimension and activity of the church's mission which seeks to offer every person, everywhere, a valid opportunity to be directly challenged by the gospel of explicit faith in Jesus Christ, with a view to embracing him as Savior, becoming a living member of his community, and being enlisted in his service of reconciliation, peace, and justice on earth. (p. 17)

Leonard and Bosch agree that both the church organization and the individual believer are included in this development of a new pattern of life and mission.

Burrill (2007) also looks at evangelism as going beyond a simple mental acceptance of the "good news" to include life transformation as a part of the body of Christ, particularly a local church. He succinctly defines evangelism as "the process of winning people to Jesus Christ and enabling them to be transformed by God into responsible church members who are ready to meet Jesus when He comes" (p. 10).

These three definitions agree that evangelism does not end with a mere acceptance of Jesus. Evangelism is not complete until the believer is progressing through the holistic process of discipleship that will result in striving to make disciples of others.

This project is completed in the context of the Seventh-day Adventist Church. Believing that the return of Jesus is very soon, the Adventist Church senses a special mission of evangelism as especially portrayed in the message of the three angels of Revelation 14. The call is to take the "everlasting gospel" to the whole world, proclaiming the life-changing power of God to transform the lives of Christians, as evidenced by keeping the commandments of God and having the faith of Jesus (Rev 14:6-12). This will be the final message to the world before the Second Coming (v. 14)

Each person's full acceptance of the gift of the gospel will be also revealed in his or her active participation in the mission of God. Successful evangelism has taken place when an individual has accepted Christ into their life, allowed the Holy Spirit to begin life changes, and has a desire to share this new excitement with those around them because of their love toward Christ.

Called to Evangelism

All Christians are called to participate in the mission of the Church. This mission is to make disciples by going to all nations and baptizing and teaching others about Jesus (Matt 28:19, 20). This "Great Commission" is the foundation of the church's purpose. As people come to believe in Jesus as their Savior, as they become disciples, they are called to make new disciples. This on-going process allowed Christianity to sweep the world and caused the rapid growth of the church (Acts 17:6).

The invitation for full participation is often referred to as the "priesthood of all believers," a concept clearly seen in 1 Peter 2:9—"But you are a chosen generation, a royal priesthood, a holy nation, His own special people, that you may proclaim the praises of Him who called you out of darkness into His marvelous light." Peter, writing to the Christian church at large (1 Pet 1:1, 2), calls for all Christians to take part in this ministry of the church. This naturally includes both young and old, and male and female.

People of all ages will be involved in sharing messages both from God and about God (Joel 2:28, 29). Joel specifically mentions "your sons and your daughters," and "your old men" and "your young men." Clearly age (or gender) is not a distinguishing factor in who is capable and called to share the gospel message. This Old Testament prophecy is repeated in the New Testament at the formation of the church as Peter preached on the day of Pentecost (Acts 2:17, 18), indicating that all Christians are still called to actively take part in the mission of the church. The addition of the phrase "in the last days" (v. 17) extends the ministry of old and young from the foundation of the church to the second coming of Jesus.

Biblical Examples

The Bible gives many examples of young people successfully participating in the mission of evangelism. Jeremiah was a young man when he received the call to serve as God's prophet. Because of his youth, he was hesitant to serve, but God responded with assurance that He would be with him and guide his words and ministry (Jer 1:4-10). Later Jeremiah spoke of his ministry as a "burning fire" that he could not hold back (20:9). He felt compelled to share the message of God regardless of age and experience.

Other examples of young people sharing in the ministry of God is seen in the lives of Ruth, Samuel, David, Joseph, Esther, and Daniel and his three friends, as well as many others. These young men and women came from a variety of backgrounds and professions, revealing that all are called to work for God.

Throughout the New Testament there are also several examples of young people actively fulfilling their role of sharing the gospel message. A young man named Timothy traveled with Paul (Acts 16:3) on his missionary journeys. As Paul mentored Timothy, he became a "fellow worker (συνεργός)" (Rom 16:21), "a beloved and faithful son (τέκνον) in the Lord, who will remind you of my ways in Christ" (1 Cor 4:17), and one who "does the work of the Lord" (16:10). Timothy was mentioned as a co-writer in the greetings of several of Paul's epistles, and served as a messenger and spokesman for Paul to the churches that they had planted (1 Thess 1:1; 3:6; 2 Thess 1:1).

Timothy was also the recipient of the two epistles that bear his name. These short letters from a mentor to a young minister contain words of advice on sharing the gospel. Paul states that even though Timothy is young (νεότης), he should not let that interfere with his ministry (1 Tim 4:12). Timothy was instructed to rightly conduct himself in the church as it is the source of sharing truth (3:15), to preach and always be ready to share God's truth (2 Tim 4:1, 2), and to "do the work of an evangelist" (εὐαγγελιστοῦ) (v. 5).

Young people must also be equipped to train others to share the gospel. This key element in the growth of the early church is found in Paul's instructions on how to make a disciple. Paul tells Timothy to take the lessons and truths that he is learning and to share them with others who will in turn share these lessons with still others (2 Tim 2:2). An ongoing mentoring and training process is established as truth and knowledge is continually passed on to the next learning generation. This is the essence of fulfilling the Gospel Commission, and this instruction was given to Timothy, a young man beginning his work of ministry.

Paul gives a clear example of the importance of mentoring young people in ministry and evangelism in his interactions with Timothy. Young men and women should be trained to do the work of evangelism by more experienced workers who can share their expertise.

The story of John Mark is another biblical example of guiding a young person into a life of active outreach. Mark went on an initial missionary journey with Paul but soon abandoned the mission (Acts 13:5, 13). After a dispute regarding Mark, Barnabas and Paul went their separate ways. Barnabas continued in ministry with Mark (15:37-39). That is the last time the actions of Barnabas are mentioned in Scripture. But at the end of his life, Paul requests that Mark come to him, indicating "he is useful to me for ministry" (2 Tim 4:11). Apparently, the mentoring of Barnabas helped young Mark to become a useful minister of the gospel.

In summary, young people in both the Old and New Testaments were given an active role in sharing God's message with the world around them. As they fulfilled this role, they were successful in telling others the truths about God. Young people will be most effective as they are taught and shown ways of telling the world about Jesus by mentors and those more experienced.

Gathering for Evangelism

This section will explore a biblical understanding of small groups and the concept of small groups as a basis for evangelism. Much has been accurately written about the relational aspect of small groups throughout scripture (Burrill, 1997; James, 2005; Johnson, 2011), but another key purpose of biblical small groups is for organization and for acts of service.

Old Testament

A concept of shared leadership for service is first seen in the Old Testament story of the Exodus. Jethro, the father-in-law of Moses, saw the burden of Moses' extreme workload and suggested a brilliant alternative model of leadership. Instead of Moses hearing the concerns of all the people, Jethro suggested he should equip leaders and set them over groups of thousands, hundreds, fifties, and tens (Exod 18:21-23). Some of these leaders functioned in groups of a smaller size. This model of group leadership appears to be primarily for the functionality of the organization rather than building relationships, and it appears to have been a great success (v. 26). Some benefits of this design were the training of leaders on multiple levels and improved community morale.

Jesus in the Gospels

In the New Testament, Jesus regularly worked with a small group of people as a basis for His ministry. Andrew and John, the very first followers of Jesus, left the crowd surrounding John the Baptist and asked Jesus where he was staying. Jesus invited them to come with Him, and they spent the day with Him (John 1:38, 39). As this small group met, disciples were made, and they immediately invited others to meet this Messiah (John 1:40, 41).

Although surrounded by the masses, Jesus soon called 12 individuals and gave them special attention. Coleman (1972) refers to this method as the "foundation" of Jesus' ministry and notes the success: "The more concentrated the size of the group being taught, the greater the opportunity for effective instruction" (p. 27). Jesus was able to model his message and mission during intensive times with a small group of people. In time, these disciples lived out these instructions and "turned the world upside down" (Acts 17:6).

After this initial group of 12 disciples, another group of 70 is gathered and sent out by Jesus (Luke 10:1, 2). This group was instructed, trained, and sent out in groups of two to tell others about the message of Jesus. Their mission was also a success, and they returned full of joy (v. 17). Serving God together with others will result in success. Success in sharing the gospel will bring joy. Joy is a key element in the development of a fulfilled Christian life (Phil 4:4; 1 Thess 5:16).

Jesus was not neglecting the crowds, but rather establishing a pattern of church organization that would reach the far corners of the earth. Burrill (1997) recognizes the continuing success of this organizational style and states that "Jesus revealed that the way to reach the masses was through small groups that were experiencing genuine community" (p. 46).

Jesus ends His earthly ministry by giving a group of disciples a Great Commission to go and make more disciples (Matt 28:19, 20; Mark 16:14-16; Luke 24:46-49). This task must have seemed impossible for a small number of uneducated, working class individuals. The disciples started this task by immediately replicating the small group model they experienced with Jesus.

The Church in Acts

The Book of Acts begins with instructions to remain in Jerusalem (Luke 24:49; Acts 1:4). The disciples prayed together waiting for the gift of the Holy Spirit that would aid them in fulfilling the Great Commission (Acts 1:8, 14; 2:1). As the gospel was preached in the power of the Spirit on the Day of Pentecost, many were baptized and the church grew. With this sudden growth, the immediate response was the formation of small groups of believers for the purpose of spiritual development. This resulted in even more numerical growth (2:42-47).

The clearest picture of small group methodology in the New Testament is found in Acts 2:42: "And they continued steadfastly in the apostles' doctrine and fellowship, in the breaking of bread, and in prayers." This verse gives insight into how the early church functioned. There were no church buildings or places for large groups of people to gather (Jeffers, 1999), so four key elements received prominence in this infant church: (a) the teaching of the apostles, (b) fellowship, (c) the breaking of bread, and (d) prayer. These four elements, and their modern equivalents, remain important foundational stones for an effective small group ministry today.

The teaching of the apostles (*τῇ διδαχῇ τῶν ἀποστόλων*) equates to the modern-day study of the Bible, which contains many of the apostles' teachings in the form of the New Testament. The Bible needs to be the foundation for learning, for ministry, and for outreach (2 Tim 3:16, 17).

Fellowship (*κοινωνίᾳ*) speaks of a communion among believers. In a society of oppression and differentiation, this building of close-knit community is of vital importance to all people, especially Millennials (Dean, 2010). Easum and Atkinson (2007) describe this type of community as more in depth than can take place in a normal church setting. Instead, it is what happens when people are able to spend time together and show care and concern for each other.

The breaking of bread (*κλάσει τοῦ ἄρτου*) can refer to the celebration of the Lord's Supper (1 Cor 11:23, 24), but it can also refer to the simple, yet intimate, act of sharing a meal together (Acts 2:46). Small groups that eat together are often able to form a close bond that will aid in their outreach efforts.

Prayer (*προσευχαῖς*) is a vital element to the small group function in the New Testament and remains of utmost importance today. It is a source of connection with God and a channel through which power flows. The church prayed and was united (Acts 1:14), the Holy Spirit was poured out and thousands were baptized (2:2, 3), they were filled with boldness to preach (4:31), new cultures received the Holy Spirit (8:15; 10:9, 31), apostles were delivered from prison (12:12; 16:25), missionaries were commissioned for new territories (13:3), deacons and elders were appointed to aid in the spread of the gospel (6:6; 14:23), and healings took place (28:8). Evangelistic small groups need this same prayer power to be truly effective today.

House Churches

Throughout much of the New Testament there are many references to *house churches*. These verses are most often in the greetings or salutations of Paul's epistles (Phil 1:2; Col 4:15; Rom 16:5; 1 Cor 16:9). The New Testament also mentions "teaching and preaching" (Acts 5:42; 20:20), and fellowship and breaking bread (2:46) from "house to house."

These verses seem to be primarily descriptive, not necessarily prescriptive. "The groups meeting in households were the basic cells of the early Christian movement" (Gehring, 2004, p. 81). Adams (2009) reflects on the growing importance of house churches as the early Christian church expands in the book of Acts and the New Testament, and also sees a renewed relevance in today's society.

"One Another" Passages

The New Testament contains over 45 "one another" passages. Categorizing these statements, Kranz (2014) shows that one-third of the these passages deal with unity in the church, one-third instructs Christians to show love to each other, and about 15% refer to the need for a humble attitude, while the remaining passages refer to miscellaneous commands. While not referring directly to small groups, the instructional theme of these passages clearly show the importance of the interpersonal relationships of the early church.

Outreach in Small Groups

The New Testament does not give a detailed description of how small groups functioned for evangelism, but there are several instances where ministry takes place in this mode. Jesus sent out the disciples two by two for their first missionary journey (Mark 6:7, Luke 10:1). The book of Acts describes Paul and his companions following a similar model (Acts 13:1-3; 15:39, 40; 20:4), while also often adding a young person to mentor along the way (Acts 12:25; 16:3). In the greetings and salutations of his epistles, Paul frequently mentions his companions, revealing that much of his time in ministry was spent in the context of a small group of believers (Rom 16:21-23; 1 Cor 1:1; Phil 1:1; 4:21). Aquila and Priscilla, a successful ministry couple, also worked with small groups of people in mentoring and training others (Acts 18:2, 18), namely Apollos, for discipleship and evangelism (v. 26).

This incidental evidence provides some direction for a theology of outreach in small groups. Groups of believers working together can be a source of support and encouragement, and can transmit experience and training to others in the group. As more individuals respond to evangelistic efforts, these groups can continue in this manner, as well as serving as a source of fellowship and community for both old and new believers.

Small Group Summary

Throughout the New Testament, small groups were one of the primary structures of church organization. These groups met in various places, from the temple courts to the local synagogue, and from private homes to riverside gathering places. Even though outreach or evangelism is generally not a specifically stated purpose of these groups, growth was still a result. The prevalent picture of missionary work in the New Testament shows a missionary like Paul, along with a group of believers, working in a city for the purpose of evangelism. While the day-to-day group dynamics are not seen in Scripture, the results of this working situation are clearly observed. As the church grew exponentially in the book of Acts, the effectiveness of this small group model is revealed.

Models of Evangelism

The Bible calls all Christians to be involved in spreading the gospel message to the ends of the earth (Matt 24:14; 28:19, 20). Throughout Scripture, there are at least two major models of letting others know about this message and the character of God. One model of sharing is by Transformational Outreach, meeting the felt needs of people. A second model of sharing is by Proclamational Outreach, preaching the Gospel of Christ to address the spiritual needs of individuals. Sometimes these two methods of evangelism are thought to be in conflict with each other, but the New Testament reveals these are actually complimentary actions.

Jesus' ministry included both the transforming of lives by meeting the needs of people around him and the proclamation of the kingdom of God. Matthew describes Jesus with a three-fold focus of preaching, teaching, and healing (Matt 4:23; 9:35). He met both physical and spiritual needs. Jesus noticed felt needs and worked to meet them: He turned water to wine (John 2:8, 9), He fed those that were hungry (Matt 14:19, 20), and He healed the sick (Mark 1:32-24). But He was also deeply concerned over spiritual challenges that people faced (Mark 2:5; Luke 19:9, 10; John 8:11, 12; 9:35-38).

Sahlin (2004) differentiates between "evangelism," which "involves bringing people to accept Christ," and "Community Service" or "Compassion Ministry," which provide services to people in the community to meet their needs (p. iii). He describes both types of ministries as being important to the function of the church. Church members of all ages can participate in both "evangelism" and "compassion ministry" in the context of small groups.

The next section will examine both Transformational Community Evangelism and the Proclamational Evangelism of Bible-based preaching.

Transformational Community Evangelism

For this study, Transformational Community Evangelism refers to the act of transformed Christians engaging the community in outreach activities for the purpose of transforming that community.

The North American Division of Seventh-day Adventists (2014) defines it this way: "Transformational evangelism is when the grace of God springs to life in the congregation and compels members to intentionally share the grace with their communities resulting in hope and wholeness for both." This needs-focused community outreach will only be successful as God's people work in harmony with God, the very source of love (1 John 4:7, 8). This can very naturally take place in a group setting.

Ultimate Source of Help—God

Old Testament prophets often proclaimed justice for all people, revealing that caring for the needs of the downtrodden originates with the very character of God. Sider (1997) ably argues that the Bible reveals God's special concern for the poor and outcast. God cares for all in need. As the Creator, God is the one who cares for the oppressed, the hungry, the prisoners, the blind, and the widows and orphans (Ps 146:6-9). The "widows and orphans" are frequently mentioned as recipients of God's attention (Deut 10:18, Ps

68:5), perhaps as a symbol of all in need. God clearly is concerned for all people, even those that society ignores. He is the source of help for those in need, and the Church, the Body of Christ working in harmony with each member taking part, is the means for this help to take place.

Incarnational Example of Help—Jesus

Jesus is the Incarnation of the Godhead on earth (Matt 1:23; John 1:1-3, 14; 14:7). Near the beginning of His ministry, Jesus quotes from Isaiah 61, announcing his Spirit-empowered mission "to preach the gospel to the poor . . . to heal the broken hearted . . . [and] to proclaim liberty" (Luke 4:18). While Jesus clearly had a preaching ministry (even mentioned in this passage), He also emphasized his ministry to the forgotten and the oppressed. Jesus healed lepers (Luke 17:12-14), spent time with tax collectors and prostitutes (Matt 9:10), and ministered to all those in need (Mark 6:34).

Jesus not only helped others Himself, but taught his followers to do the same. His teachings instructed disciples that they are to be the "salt of the earth" and the "light of the world" because their good works would bring glory to God in heaven (Matt 5:13-16). Jesus declares that the very foundation of following God is seen by showing love to God and by loving "your neighbor as yourself" (22:37-40). Jesus' interaction with the Samaritan women (John 4) emphasizes the need to help even those pushed to the periphery of importance by society.

As Christians proclaiming the soon return of Jesus, these instructions to care for the needs of others take on extra importance. After proclaiming to the disciples the signs revealing the nearness of His return (Matt 24), Jesus shared three parables to teach disciples how to live in light of the second coming (chap. 25). Jesus talked about being prepared for his coming even when we get spiritually drowsy, and about using all our gifts and talents for his glory. Then he shared the Parable of the Sheep and Goats (vv. 31-44). In this parable, only one thing separates these two groups representing the righteous and the wicked. Significantly the thing that separates the groups is how they treat "the least of these," those that are hungry, thirsty, naked, or in prison. The teaching of Jesus echoes the teaching of the Old Testament and reflects His own life. The act of loving others reveals a Christian's connection and acceptance of the grace of God.

Ongoing Community of Help—God's People

God's people are called to care for those that have any needs, including physical, social, health, and economic. In modern terms, these are often referred to as "felt needs." Isaiah 58 begins with an appeal to challenge the Israelites regarding their sins, to "cry aloud" (v. 1). In this passage, the preaching is not evangelistic, but is directed toward God's people to get them to serve those in need. God is not ready to accept the people's worship and fasting because of their sins, which includes exploitation of the social outcasts (v. 3). The actions that God will accept in this case are meeting those felt needs: "to loose the bonds of wickedness," to feed the hungry, to care for the poor, and to clothe the naked (vv. 6, 7).

Other prophets also show that God is not interested in the forms of worship that the people are offering Him absent a caring attitude (Mic 6:6, 7). Worship is more than going through the motions, more than showing up, more than looking the part. Worshippers show their inner heart by the way that others are treated, in this case to "do justly, to love mercy, and to walk humbly with your God" (v. 8).

The apostles practiced their Christianity by meeting the needs of others. Immediately after the exponential growth of the church started, the believers were making sure that the needs of everyone was met, even going so far as selling their belongings and property (Acts 2:44, 45; 4:32-35). These instances appear to refer to believers, Christians taking care of the needs of other Christians. While this does not refer to taking care of the needs of those who were not part of the church, this attitude of love and caring surely was a significant factor in the rapid growth of the church.

In Acts 6, church organization was modified for the purpose of meeting physical needs. Deacons were selected and ordained to engage in the work of ministry (feeding and caring for widows) so the apostles could continue in "prayer and . . . the ministry of the word" (Acts 6:4). As needs were met, people were more open to receiving the gospel message. This change in organization allowed the gospel to spread even more and the church to continue its rapid growth (v. 7).

Throughout his missionary journeys, Paul collected money for the aid of those suffering from famine in Jerusalem (1 Cor 16:1; 2 Cor 8:4; Rom 15:26). James expands on the theme of a "faith that works" by stating that the purest religion is exhibited by visiting those in need, particularly "orphans and widows" (Jas 1:27). The apostles both taught and exhibited a desire to help those in need. Christians today must take an active role in recognizing needs around them, and taking actions to meet those needs based on the resources available in the local church.

Summary

Throughout the Old and New Testament God's people were expected to reveal God's love by caring for the needs of people around them. Recognizing that all people are created in the image of God, Christians of all ages, working in community with each other, are to exhibit that love by recognizing what can be done to help others, and by doing all that is possible to fulfill those needs through their actions. This is the result of God's love shining through their life.

Proclamational Evangelism

While the major focus of this study is Transformational Evangelism, the prominence of Proclamational Evangelism in Scripture is seen as complimentary in nature and will also be briefly examined. Even with the theme of serving others being so prevalent throughout the scriptures, without a doubt one of the primary ways of sharing the Gospel in the New Testament Church was through preaching.

The Ministry of Jesus

Preaching, along with teaching and healing, was part of the regular pattern of Jesus' ministry (Matt 9:35). It has been shown that Jesus focused on a small group of disciples, but He also had an effective preaching ministry (Matt 5:1, 2; 14:13; 15:32). Large crowds came to listen to Him, and were amazed at His message (7:28, 29). Jesus took an active role in publicly proclaiming the message of the kingdom of God (4:17).

The Apostles

The apostles mirrored the ministry of Jesus by also placing an emphasis on preaching. From the opening sermon on the day of Pentecost (Acts 2:15) the gospel message is shared. The gospel message is preached in the temple (v. 46), in the synagogue (17:1, 2; 19:8), in the market place (16:19), and the places of learning (17:22). Burrill (2014) indicates that the preaching in the New Testament was almost exclusively evangelistic in nature (for an in-depth study on preaching in the New Testament, see pp. 12-24).

The public proclamation of the gospel in newly visited towns was a key element in the church planting movement that takes place throughout the books of Acts. As mentioned earlier, preaching was not an exclusive element of ministry, but served in a complimentary role along with the disciple-making process of small groups. The public preaching of the gospel is powerful for decisions and inspiration (Acts 2:37), while the believers gathering in small groups was a source for growth and personal ministry to happen (Acts 2:42).

A brief look at two key passages reveals more insight. Paul asks, "How shall they believe in Him of whom they have not heard? And how shall they hear without a preacher? And how shall they preach unless they are sent?" (Rom 10:14, 15). This indicates a need for public preaching by revealing a logical order in the process of proclaiming, hearing, and believing. If preaching is neglected, opportunities to share the gospel will be missed.

Paul instructs the young minister, Timothy, to always be ready to "preach the Word" (2 Tim 4:2). This preaching is to "convince, rebuke, [and] exhort, with all longsuffering and teaching." In the context of Timothy's continuing ministry in Ephesus (1 Tim 1:3), this concept of preaching is an ongoing means of proclaiming the full message of Jesus and His love to reach a community. An active, growing church will need to have positive opportunities to proclaim the message of Jesus to non-believers. In the ministry of Jesus and the apostles, public preaching had a prominent and important position. It was effective as many people heard and believed. New believers accepted the message and lives were changed. In the epistles, evidence is seen that instruction was given for the ongoing proclamation of the good news of Jesus as new churches and new church leaders are raised up.

Complimentary Ministry

Both Transformational and Proclamational Outreach are important elements of evangelism that can be practiced in small group settings by young and old Christians. While some ministries may focus on either of these aspects, a well-rounded plan of evangelism will include both. As the crowds came to Jesus and the apostles for healing, their close proximity and gratefulness allowed the gospel message to be preached and accepted.

In the same way, as the felt needs of modern communities are discovered and met through compassion ministries, an avenue will be opened through these relationships to share the Gospel message in order also to meet the spiritual needs of those who have been helped. Those helped who have had their felt needs met will be more likely to respond to invitations for Bible study or to church and other meetings specifically designed for the Proclamation of the gospel, complete with invitations to follow Jesus.

Summary

The New Testament contains at least two models of outreach for all Christians to participate in.. Transformational Evangelism results in meeting the felt needs of people in the community. An equally important model is Proclamational Evangelism, the public preaching of the gospel. These two models are not contradictory, but work well together throughout the New Testament story, often seen taking place in small groups. Therefore, an evangelism model today will work best when it includes both Transformational and Proclamational elements to work together and impact a larger number of people. A biblically sound outreach model will have these two complimentary components working in conjunction with each other as a foundation for ministry opportunities.

Summary of Theological Reflection

A theology of Millennial involvement in small groups for transformational evangelism has been explored from a survey of the Old and New Testament. This evangelism refers to the invitation for individuals to not only accept Jesus as their Savior, but to also be actively engaged in the mission of the church.

In this reflection, three elements have emerged that provide a framework for this project: (a) the participants in evangelism, (b) the gathering for evangelism, and (c) the models of evangelism. God calls all Christians to participate in these activities of outreach. Evidence is given that young people are included in this call, and have been successful participants throughout the Old and New Testament.

Following the example of Jesus, the early church gathered together in small groups for outreach. These groups were for more than fellowship, but also served as units of mentoring and training of church members, both young and old. These units were able to reach out the community around them and exhibit God's love.

Biblical records specify at least two methods of evangelism. Transformational evangelism involves meeting the felt needs of people in the local community. God is the ultimate source of that help, Jesus is the incarnational example of help, and the church is the ongoing community of help. This allows Christians to not only talk about God's love, but to exhibit His love to others. Transformational evangelism needs to work in conjunction with proclamational evangelism to be most effective. Proclamational evangelism allows individuals to hear the truths of scripture and invites them to follow this God of love with their heart and life. Both of these methods of evangelism can take place in the small group setting.

The ongoing challenge of this project will be to encourage young people to recognize their call to participate in the mission of God and to respond by taking part in small groups that will provide places of encouragement and training to be involved in transformational community outreach. In Chapter 3, literature will be reviewed in these areas, and this plan will be implemented in Chapter 4.

CHAPTER 3

LITERATURE RELATING TO MILLENNIAL INVOLVEMENT

IN TRANSFORMATIONAL EVANGELISM

There is a wide variety of literature related to Millennial involvement in community outreach, or Transformational Evangelism. Many subject areas are related to this research, including characteristics and attitudes of the Millennial generation, varieties of outreach-oriented ministry philosophies, practical methodologies of community outreach and social interaction, and training methodologies to engage Millennials in outreach. Each of these subject areas has a large range of available literature. Study for this Doctor of Ministry project will investigate the scriptural and theological basis for involving young people in ministry, community transformational outreach, and training and equipping young people via outreach-oriented small groups. The literature considered for this review will be limited primarily to those published between 2008 and 2013, except for a few earlier works that are seen as important for these subjects.

This literature review will focus on works that look at four major subject areas. First, research on the characteristics of the Millennial Generation and their attitude toward the church and spiritual matters. Second, professional works referencing outreach-oriented ministries show that an outward focus is vital for reaching the community. Third, practical works insight into community-based outreach suggest a need to invest time and energy in discovering community needs. Fourth, professional works suggest evangelistic training methodologies for Millennials should include reflection, community, and small groups.

This survey reveals that Millennials are a gifted generation with a desire to work together and to make a difference in the world. Outreach philosophies show that the church must begin focusing on meeting community needs by taking the time to investigate and learn what those needs are. Millennials can be trained to take part in reaching their community through mentoring and small groups. This outreach will result in the strengthening of their personal walk with God.

Studies on the Millennial Generation

The first section will look at various studies on the characteristics of the Millennial Generation. These include scholarly works, reports of surveys, and studies on members of this generation. This section will first look at general characteristics of the Millennial Generation, and then will look at Millennial attitudes toward the church and spirituality.

General Characteristics of the Millennial Generation

Howe and Strauss (2000), scholars of several various generational studies, did much of the early work in studying the Millennial Generation, including coining the term "Millennial" that is used in this study. Their early investigations into Millennial characteristics seem to be the most quoted studies in subsequent works and are therefore seen as very influential. They indicate that the Millennial Generation refers to those born between 1982 and 2002. This generation is poised to be the next great generation and will likely resist some of the negative imagery seen in Generation X. Howe and Strauss discovered seven core traits of the Millennial Generation: Special, Sheltered, Confident, Team-Oriented, Conventional, Pressured, and Achieving.

Later studies, such as Howe and Nadler (2010), confirm the accuracy of the earlier predictions of Howe and Strauss and look at the influence this generation is having on the current workplace as they move from college to the workforce. Millennials are known for their confidence, for doing well in team settings, and for being very teachable. Howe and Nadler also note that some in society see challenges in working with Millennials because many of the members of this generation are not risk-takers and often do not show much initiative.

Winograd and Hais (2011) found that this generation has the potential to be very influential in both American society and the world as a whole. While agreeing with Howe and Strauss that Millennials thrive in team settings, they also note that this generation is very idealistic and wants to make an impact. They want their lives, their jobs, and their play to have meaning and to make a difference in the world.

The tendencies of the Millennial Generation are similar around the western world. Studies done in Australia (Mason, Singleton, & Webber, 2007) and Europe (Appleton, 2012) correlate well with the predictions of Howe and Strauss and the more recent American studies.

Although most authors confirm the predictions of Howe and Strauss, Agati (2012) disputes the generalization of the source of Millennial characteristics. While seeing many similarities in the characteristics themselves, Agati sees other sources for those characteristics besides simply being of age during a certain generation. These other sources include each individual's family, education, and religious background.

Elmore (2010) agrees with Howe and Strauss about the positive outlook for those in the early part of the Millennial Generation. But he observes a change for the worse in the younger portion of that group. He coined the term "Generation iY," referring specifically to those born from 1990-2002 (p. 32). Many in Generation iY have been raised with overbearing, overprotective, helicopter parents in a world consumed by technology. This generation has the desire to change the world, but does not have the skills or the patience to carry through with these tasks, leading some to refer to them as "slacktivists" (p. 27).

Spiritual Characteristics of the
Millennial Generation

Several authors have observed specific characteristics in how the Millennial Generation relate to spirituality and the church. These characteristics influence the manner in which youth and young adults will be involved in gospel outreach.

Millennials and the Church

In his book *SoulTsunami*, Sweet (1999) was one of the first to write about post-modern culture in relation to the church. He sees the post-modern culture of the Millennial Generation as being comparable to an earthquake in the changes being brought rapidly into culture and into the church. These changes are so many and so vast that the church will have to shift methodologies to reach this generation while at the same time preserving the gospel message. Sweet suggests that to reach this group, teaching must be EPIC (Experiential, Participatory, Image-driven, and Connected).

Moralistic Therapeutic Deism

In *Soul Searching: The Religious and Spiritual Lives of the American Teenager*, Smith and Denton (2005) looked closely at the research of the National Study of Youth and Religion (NSYR). This study looked at the religious lives of thousands of teens, many of which were studied over a longitudinal period. The NSYR is perhaps the most important religious study of young people in the last 10 years and its major finding is quoted in many subsequent books.

This primary finding of Smith and Denton is the idea of Moralistic Therapeutic Deism (MTD), a concept first developed in their book. In recent years, this is still seen as the prevalent idea held among Christian teenagers (as well as the church at large). MTD is summed up with five statements:

1. A God exists who created and orders the world and watches over human life on earth.
2. God wants people to be good, nice, and fair to each other, as taught in the Bible and by most world religions.
3. The central goal of life is to be happy and to feel good about oneself.
4. God does not need to be particularly involved in one's life except when God is needed to resolve a problem.
5. Good people go to Heaven when they die. (pp. 162, 163)

Because the concept of MTD is so prevalent among youth and adults, it will continue to greatly shape the future of the church in America and the world.

Spiritual, But Not Religious

Kimball (2007) indicates that many young adults are leaving the church for a variety of reasons. Many in today's post-modern culture are not fond of the "institution" of the church. This has given rise to the popular phrase, "spiritual but not religious," indicating that they appreciate the teachings of Jesus (or at least the idea of Jesus), but they do not like what the church has become—in their opinion, fake, focused on money, and self-centered.

Rainer and Rainer (2011) go a step beyond Kimball and have found that most Millennials do not talk about, or even think of, any spirituality, including Christianity. It is not that they are opposed to the Church, it is that "most Millennials don't think about religious matters at all" (p. 21).

In their recent study, Winograd and Hais (2011) have found that many Millennials are believers, but they are less likely than previous generations to be part of a specific religious faith (p. 206). They believe some of the basic understandings of the spiritual movement they grew up in, but do not see the need of being an active part in a faith community.

In the 2012 Millennial Values Survey (Jones, Cox, & Banchoff), statistics revealed that 58% of college-age Millennials felt that Christianity is relevant to their life. The statistics also revealed that while 76% felt that modern-day Christianity "has good values and principles, about 60% feel that Christianity is 'judgmental' and 'hypocritical'" (p. 32). Millennials want Christian principles without the negatives that have become part of the institutionalized church.

Differing from Kimball and others, Smith and Denton (2005) believe that the concept of "spiritual, but not religious," while used by so many authors, is not truly understood by teenagers themselves. They just do not grasp the concept of this phrase to which others are referring. Smith and Snell (2009) agree with this sentiment, indicating that this statement "may be overestimated by survey research" (p. 296).

Implications

The Millennial generation has several positive characteristics, which indicate a teachable attitude and a desire to do positive things, but in general, have an indifferent attitude toward the church. This dichotomy must be dealt with while training Millennials to be involved in outreach.

Types of Community Outreach Philosophies

The second category of literature that was investigated focused on discovering several varieties of outreach-oriented ministry philosophies. These works look at different theologies of outreach, as well as differing practical methods of making a difference in the community.

Missional

A recent, but popular, philosophy of ministry is referred to as "missional" church. While some like Hill (2012) are beginning to look more deeply at the theology and ecclesiology of the missional church movement, many books about missional church reflect a more practical focus.

Many authors, including Drane (2008) and McNeal (2009), see the need of the church to develop a mission mentality for Western culture. There are many differing groups living in this secular, post-modern society: the desperately poor, hedonists, traditionalist, spiritual but not religious, secularists, and the apathetic. Each of these will require the church to leave its walls and to minister in specific and unique ways in that community of belief.

Roxburgh and Boren (2009) agree in seeing the West as the new mission field. While admitting that it is difficult to define just what a missional church is and how it functions, the authors state that in this new Western mission field, "we need local churches to become mission agencies in their neighborhoods and communities" (p. 68). Each missional community of faith can look to see how God is already in action in their neighborhood.

Putnam (2008) adds to the missional discussion by challenging not just churches, but individuals to grow in their walk with God and to become an active missionary by going out into the community and bringing new people into contact with the community of faith.

Halter and Smay (2010) critique several differing philosophies of ministry. They find that mega and multi-site churches spend large amounts of money on staff and buildings, but often fail to mobilize church members into ministry. Organic churches suffer from a lack of structure and the challenge to truly inspire worshippers in small, house settings. Instead of a competition between a Modalic structure (focused on those already in the church) and a Sodalic structure (focused completely on those outside the church), they argue that there must be a combination of Modality and Sodality working together. This provides a way to engage church members in ministry in the community, and provides a structured opportunity for spiritual growth and inspiring worship.

By looking at missional ideas from both theological and practical perspectives, Keller (2012) agrees with Halter and Smay in seeing a need for a multi-focus ministry. Keller also notes additional important aspects of outreach. The church must be gospel-centered and have as its primary mission the sharing of the message of the cross of Christ. To successfully carry out this mission, the local church must be engaged in its local community. This requires sharing the gospel personally, and modeling the gospel through acts of service that meet the communities needs.

Development of Outreach Ideas

Over the last ten years, different philosophies of missional orientation have been developed. In many ways they are very similar in their methodology, each emphasizing the importance of an outward focus for the church, but sometimes differing in how the approach is carried out in practical life.

Organic Church

Neil Cole (2005) utilizes the term Organic Church to describe a way of taking Christ to the community (as opposed to inviting the community to the church). Organic church is about "the presence of Jesus among His people called out as a spiritual family to pursue His mission on this planet" (p. 53). Witness is not about a one-hour service on the weekend, but about intentionally living a life for Christ and for others, by finding out where in the community are the people most likely to receive Christ.

Simple Discipleship

Rainer and Geiger (2006) ask the church to move away from complicating structures to a simple means of operating in order to make a kingdom difference. Like

Cole, this simple structure is more focused on the community and less focused on maintaining buildings and programs that are primarily for people who are already members of the church. They also see the importance of simple missional communities making a difference in the community.

Externally Focused Church

Swanson and Rusaw (2010) indicate that churches need to change the question they are trying to answer. Instead of asking how to be the best church IN the community, churches should start asking how to be the best church FOR the community (p. 3). Because society practices a mobile lifestyle, the church no longer needs to exist in only one centralized place. Agreeing with both Cole and Rainer and Geiger, an externally focused church will be both simple and organic, focusing on the community as opposed to those already part of the church. A key idea for this church will be "authentic service that meets real human needs" (p. 51).

Graceful Evangelism

Adeney (2010) looks at a theology and practice of Graceful Evangelism. She sees evangelistic outreach as being centered around an "Abundant Life." This means that as people live an abundant life in Christ, they can aide in bringing an abundant life to those around them. A Christian should minister to others in the same way that Jesus did: healing the sick, assisting the poor, and associating with those on the outskirts of society. As a church is making a plan for evangelism, members should notice what needs are present in the community, and act on those concerns while partnering with other groups that are working for the same cause.

Transformational Church

Stetzer and Rainer (2010) look at what characteristics were present in churches that were involved in transforming communities. Transformational churches are involved in justice mission work, but for the purpose of telling a lost soul about Jesus. There should not be a dichotomy between proclamation of the gospel and justice, but a partnership. As Christians engage in serving others, they draw into relational engagement, which leads to opportunities to share the gospel (Stetzer & Rainer, 2010, p. 69).

Implications

Literature in recent years reveals the importance of the local church taking the focus off those that are already church members and looking for ministry opportunities in the community among the unchurched.

Studies in Community Development

The third category of literature focuses on the topic of understanding the community in which ministry is to take place. The focus is on books and studies that deal with the practical implications of discovering community needs as well as church strengths, and finding ways to be engaged in transformational outreach.

Discovering Community Needs

In *Understanding Your Community*, Sahlin (2004) lays out a very detailed methodology of getting to know the community. This is a very important book because of the detailed description on finding and interpreting information. Although some of the methodology is now dated (i.e., CD-ROMs), the concepts are still valuable for discovering needs and target population. The study shows how to look at demographics, church strengths, and community needs, as well as visualizing a community by driving or walking the streets, and how to make sense of the data that is discovered.

In *Breaking the Missional Code* Stetzer and Putnam (2006) look theologically at the importance of understanding the community, and then utilizing the best methods to interact with the people in it. It is not enough to copy the methods of other successful churches. These churches are successful because they have used techniques to meet the specific needs of their specific communities. Each church must discover the "code" of its own community. Steps to understand the culture include: looking at census information and studying demographics, talking to local experts (government officials, community service leaders, business leaders, etc.), as well as long-term residents. Their philosophy is based on: "How we do church is grounded in Scripture but applied in culture" (Stetzer & Putnam, 2006, p. 53).

Crocker (2008) states that ministering to needs can cause community transformation. He notes the importance of compassion ministry, particularly to those who are poor. Crocker observes an additional element that arises from compassion ministry. Not only are the poor helped and a way is open to share the gospel, but also church members who are helping will see their own spiritual walk grow; therefore, the compassion ministry has a circular effect of causing community transformation, which causes growth in the individual church members, who then are inspired to serve more in the community, and so on.

Black and Harold (2010) expand on this idea by stating that felt needs must be met in order to open up opportunities to share the gospel. This study argues that the major felt need throughout world is the scourge of poverty, and that the church has a biblical mandate to begin to equip people to rise up from a state of poverty. This change can only happen through developmental projects that will cause community transformation. At the same time, the church must look for opportunities to share the message of the cross.

Roxburgh (2011) continues the missional discussion stating the need to develop teams of believers to walk through a neighborhood and see it in a new way. One way to view the community is to see what God is already doing in the neighborhood and to seek to join in that action.

Community Transformation

In a study of urban Seventh-day Adventist churches, Sahlin (2007) has found that there is a definite correlation "between community service and church growth" (p. 100). It is unclear if this growth results from conversions taking place, or from people transferring to churches that are involved in the community. He shows that community service-type transformational outreach is desperately needed. These ministries not only meet the needs of the community, but also are an important part of a church-growth strategy. In the urban areas, some of the major needs involved ministries to the youth, to the aged, and for drug and alcohol problems. Each local church must find the needs of their own community, but as they meet those needs through transformational, incarnational ministry, the church will grow.

Pauline (2008) also recognizes the relational aspects of community transformation. Outreach will happen best when it is looked at relationally over the long term by meeting felt needs in the community and workplace as opposed to only behind the walls of the church. Pauline has found that this type of outreach will not be quick, but will take a long-term investment, probably three to five years. Community surveys, interviews, and conversations with community leaders are a good way to begin. A "Random Acts of Kindness" ministry, meeting community needs with no strings attached, can begin to reach a community and build excitement and enthusiasm among church members at the same time. The local church is not the goal of this type of outreach, but it is the instrument that will be used (Pauline, 2008 p. 126).

Gortner (2008) agrees with Pauline in his understanding of getting to know the community, but he sees "Transforming Evangelism" as more than getting people into church pews, and even more than being involved in social ministry. For Gortner, evangelism entails contacting others relationally and "creating space in which God's good news can be told, shared, and revealed" (p. 42). This can be done by getting to know the community, not so much through demographics, but by talking and listening to the people in the neighborhood.

Searcy and Henson (2009), building on the earlier work of Sjogren (2003), see the importance of "Servant Evangelism," which is "showing God's love by meeting practical needs while at the same time inviting someone to church" (p. 68). This is an excellent way for young people to be actively involved in reaching the community.

Burrill (2009) also recognizes that part of a church's outreach plan should include meeting the needs of people in the community. This includes ministry to the poor, but should also include meeting "Felt Needs," which could include basic health teaching, marriage enrichment, and Finance and Budget seminars. As important as small groups and community service are, Burrill strongly states that "there has to be some format for teaching the Adventist message" (p. 29) for the gospel to be clearly communicated and for the church to grow.

As mentioned earlier, Stetzer and Rainer (2010) look at transformational churches as working with a combination of community service and gospel proclamation. "The engagement in compassion ministries did not serve as an end to itself, but a way to communicate the reason for the service—namely the message of redemption in Christ" (Stetzer & Rainer, 2010, p. 203). They see a "transformational loop" of three parts: (a) Discern (mission mentality), (b) Embrace (vibrant leadership, relational intentionality, prayerful dependence), and (c) Engage (worship, community, mission) (p. 33).

McNeal (2013) agrees that Christians (as well as non-Christians) must be involved in their community. He shows how the church has gifts and talents that will meet many needs in the neighborhood around them, but too often the church is focused only on itself. As the church begins to serve, needs will be met, and church members will grow spiritually as they put their talents to use in serving others.

Implications

For a church to make a difference in the community, it must be involved in meeting the needs of the community. That can only take place as time is taken to interact with the neighborhood and discover what those needs are.

Training Millennials for Transformational Outreach

The fourth section of literature reviewed focuses on the training of Millennials for transformational outreach. This section first looks at why the church needs to train

Millennials for this type of outreach. This is followed by a look at some methodologies for training this generation.

Why Train Millennials?

Spiritual Growth

Smith and Denton (2005) have found that the teens that are more involved in serving their community tend to be those that are more actively engaged in religious life (p. 231). This characteristic continues into the young adult years of Millennials, as confirmed by Smith and Snell (2009).

Sherr, Garland, and Wolfer (2007) wondered if "community service contributes to a more active life of faith and connections to congregational life, or is it simply that those teenagers active in congregational life have more opportunity to engage in community service programs" (p. 46). This study found that when teens are involved in community service activities, they are more likely to develop a personal spiritual life that is meaningful. The results indicate that community service events and activities should be a major part of the training of youth.

In the book *Almost Christian*, Dean (2010) continues the exploration of the NSYR and looks at possible solutions to the Moralistic Therapeutic Deism (MTD) discovered by Smith and Denton. She states, "The missionary nature of the church rules out Moralistic Therapeutic Deism as a substitute for the Christian faith" (pp. 64, 65). In her desire to combat this prevalent idea of MTD, Dean looks at the service expectation found in the Mormon Church and sees transferable ideas. All Christians, young and old, must be taking part in the mission of the church to reach out into the community. Dean states:

> A missional imagination assumes that young people take part in the church's mission – that every Christian teenager is a missionary called to translate the gospel across boundaries, not because she is capable or even interested, but because she is baptized and is therefore sent into the world as Christ's envoy. (p. 97)

Kinnaman and Hawkins (2011) look at reasons why Millennial Christians are leaving the church and what can be done. They observe that 59% of young adult Christians have dropped out. It is easy to get discouraged with statistics like these, but the authors point out that this also means that 41% of young adult Christians have not dropped out. Their research has found that while this age group is not likely to share their faith with others, they are interested in serving others. They explain that Millennials "do not believe that evangelism can be separated from action" (p. 177). Young adults that are in the church are interested in making a difference, but feel that "evangelism must connect to actions on behalf of others" (p. 177).

Kinnaman and Hawkins also note a potential danger in this attitude that resonates with Stallard (2011). This danger is in focusing so much on action that the message of a crucified Savior is pushed aside. The church needs to develop a grace-filled way to interact and connect with non-Christians. One of the suggested means of meeting this goal is for churches to partner the experience and wisdom of older generations with the energy and desire to serve the younger generation. This will move the church from compartmentalizing different age groups to fully developing the potential of the church while truly training the younger generations.

In a more recent study, the Barna Group (2013a) reveals findings that disagree with this potential danger. This study (of which Kinnaman has a part) discovered that active evangelism is actually on the rise among Millennials. One explanation given is that since there are fewer Christians among the Millennial Generation, those that remain may be more motivated to share their faith with their peers. Some have been worried that this generation is too focused on social justice, but instead of focusing simply on meeting physical needs this study suggests that more and more Millennials are also sharing the gospel message.

The implications of this is that the more young people are involved in the outreach focus of their church, the more engaged they will personally be with the spiritual focus of the church.

Millennial Desire to Make a Difference

In a Baylor University study, Garland and Edmonds (2007) show that young people (in fact, most age groups of church members) have a high desire for the church to help them reach others in the community. In other words, the desire is there to make a difference; they just need some guidance in how to turn that into a reality.

Whitehead and Boyd (2008) also note that Millennials are interested in social action in the community. A survey of Adventist young adults indicates that service and social action are important indicators when choosing a church. "This age group is looking for integration between biblical teachings and lifestyle; they want to make a difference" (p. 17). Young people should be given the opportunity to serve with adults and be partners in the ministry (as opposed to simply being the objects of ministry).

Winograd and Hais (2011) show that from a very young age, Millennials have been trained to work together to solve problems in society, and are very likely to take part in activities for the purpose of making a difference (p. 226).

How to Train Millennials for
Transformational Outreach

Elmore (2013) explores the iY Generation as an active part of the workforce. He sees important elements in educating and training this generation. This group learns through practical hands-on experiences followed by reflection and learning. They desire to be part of a team or community, working together. They also are helped by having a more experienced person (often older) working beside them instead of just sitting and listening to a lecture. Through a mix of generations working on practical outreach skills, Generation iY will most effectively be involved in life-long learning.

Small Groups

Easum and Atkinson (2007) indicate that the focus of small groups should be on fellowship and community. In their model, small groups are not a method for church growth, but are one of the best means to retaining members and assisting in individual spiritual growth.

With a similar understanding of small group dynamics, Kirk et al. (2009) describes Bible study as the main characteristic of a small group ministry. They feel that this form of group activity will help to meet individual needs of the community. This type of "transformational" group emphasizes the transformation of the group members, but also recognizes that mission-oriented activities are a part of individual growth.

Engelmann (2010), agreeing with these writers, also sees the key element of a small group to be the transforming of group members. This spiritual growth will take place through fellowship and community as described in "Emmaus Road Groups" that revolve around authentic sharing and humble surrender to God.

Johnson (2011) goes beyond this understanding of small groups. While seeing the major method of small groups as including inductive Bible study, Johnson purposes the function of groups to revolve around building relationships, specifically the four key relationships of (a) God-to-person, (b) person-to-God, (c) person-to-person, and (d) person-to-world (p. 35). While evangelism is a part of this, the primary function is for community.

Petty's (2007) findings on small groups have a different focus. Petty emphasizes "externally-focused small groups." These small groups serve as a catalyst for community outreach by encouraging groups to discover outreach projects together and then serve together on a regular basis. This will aid in the spiritual growth of the group members as well as bless a city beyond what each member could do individually.

Burrill has written extensively on church growth and small groups in the Seventh-day Adventist Church. In *How to Grow an Adventist Church* (2009), he brings many ideas together. Burrill reiterates the importance of equipping lay members for ministry and member involvement in small groups. As has been a part of the Adventist church from its earliest days, these small groups should be formed for the purpose, at least in part, of serving others. As they meet the needs of the community, group members can be trained to find ways to work together to reach others.

In more recent research, Latini (2011) supports the findings of Burrill. While recognizing that most individuals participating in small groups receive some personal benefit, Latini states that a major finding of her research shows that "well-developed groups . . . propel their members into encounters with . . . the non-Christian, the marginalized, and the lonely" (p. 67). As individuals participate in small groups, they are more likely, and better able, to share their faith and to be aware of the needs around them. These mission activities include both meeting felt needs as well are more direct evangelistic actions.

While many small group proponents see them as places for deep relational growth and intimacy, Searcy (2008) sees small groups as places to make friends with people in a setting that encourages Bible study, fellowship, and service. These small groups are different from typical small groups in that they are large (20 people), short-term (10-12 weeks), and interest-based. This small group cycle tends toward leadership development through apprentice/assistant leaders and group growth (more groups with each subsequent cycle). An important element involves groups being involved together in service activities.

Disagreeing with Searcy, Gladen (2011) suggests that groups should not be based on common affinities or ministries, but should instead be based on the five biblical purposes of fellowship, discipleship, ministry, evangelism, and worship. These purposes were first suggested by Warren (1995). Gladen and Warren recognize healthy small groups as being a key element in producing both a healthy church and healthy church members.

Cowin (2011) studied the practical effectiveness of small groups in a local church setting. His findings support Burrill and Petty in their understanding of small groups for training of evangelistic methods. The groups are also used as a place for accountability to living a missional lifestyle.

Ferguson and Ferguson (2010) also see the importance of small groups in developing mature Christians. They see three segments of the Christian life:

(a) celebration, (b) connection, and (c) contribution (p. 93). Small groups are helpful for each of these segments as they celebrate members' relationship with God, connect with others in the group/church, and contribute by making a difference in the world.

In their most recent book, Stetzer and Geiger (2014) show the importance of small groups in Christian discipleship. Integral parts of effective small group ministry include serving God and serving others, and opportunities to share one's faith. They even talk about a 1-4-1 rhythm of group community as a regular part of small group interaction: 1 social activity, 4 group meetings, and 1 service activity (p. 35).

Mentoring

Decker (2007) looks at Millennial college students and their attitude toward overseas mission. The Millennials are being motivated to serve others primarily through a "worship-centered motivation" (p. 2) and the personal self-awareness that has come through Bible study and prayer. The author sees a great potential in the Millennial generation, but they must be encouraged and trained in different ways than the generations that have come before. Millennials are looking for personal mission training through mentors, dialog, and interaction with experts and with peers.

Kidder (2011) looks at four important elements for growing Adventist churches. While his ideas agree with Burrill, Kidder also notes that the top ingredient for church growth is continued Faith-based Optimism. Other key elements include prayer, getting young people involved, and leaders training and mentoring lay people so that more people will be involved in sharing their faith. This outreach is most efficient when it involves interacting with people that are already known to church members ("oikos") and meeting personal needs that are noticed.

O'Malley and Williams (2012) note that Millennials that are flourishing in emotional, social, and psychological well-being are more likely to grow as leaders. Millennial leadership training should include programs designed to increase the potential to flourish. Examples of this would be activities to increase inclusion of all, reflection exercises that integrate values, and engaging in positive civic activities. Mentoring and group exercises will also help Millennials to grow in leadership areas.

On another important note, Creps (2008) shows the importance of Reverse Mentoring. In most training, it is the older teaching the younger, but reverse mentoring acknowledges that in the current, rapidly changing culture there are several areas, including technology and current cultural trends, where the younger generation can teach the older. Perhaps the greatest benefit of this mind-set is the multi-generational mix that will result from this type of service, resulting in mutual respect and trust.

Active Learning and Reflection

A study of Millennial college students by Smith (2010) showed that service-learning, although developed for previous generations, is still effective today. Service-based educational opportunities really started in the 1980s and 1990s. Millennials have grown up being involved in community service opportunities from the earliest age and at levels unprecedented for previous generations. Service-learning provides an experience and is most effective when it includes an opportunity for reflection on the experience. Students in the Millennial generation continue to grow in community awareness and a desire to do good as they participate in service-learning activities.

Implications

It is important for Millennials to be trained for service. This generation has a desire to be involved in activities that make a difference in the world around them. It has been shown that as Millennials are involved in outreach they grow spiritually and are more engaged in church. Characteristics of the Millennial Generation indicate that small groups for community and service, mentoring relationships, and active learning with reflection are important ways for this generation to be trained to be involved in community outreach. Mentoring and active learning can very naturally take place within a small group setting.

Brief Survey of the Writings of Ellen White

Ellen White is one of the co-founders of the Seventh-day Adventist Church. Because the Seventh-day Adventist Church recognizes a special importance in her instructions, a brief survey of the topics previously examined will be considered from her writings.

Ellen White repeatedly prompted Seventh-day Adventist Christians to be actively engaged in outreach. Participants in this evangelism included all members, including young people. "Every church member should be engaged in some line of service for the Master" (1905, p. 149).

In fact, young people are to be a leading source of taking the gospel to the whole word. "With such an army of workers as our youth, rightly trained, might furnish, how soon the message of a crucified, risen, and soon-coming Saviour might be carried to the whole world" (White, 1903, p. 271). As young people are rightly trained and equipped for ministry, they can be a powerful force for evangelism.

This service will not only aid in the growth of the church, but also in the spiritual growth of individual members. White (1911) writes, "Strength to resist evil is best gained through aggressive service" (p. 105). A young person's spiritual connection with God will be made stronger as they engage in outreach.

Ellen White also echoed the importance of gathering in small groups for evangelism. Adventist history uses terms like companies, social meetings, and bands of Christian service (Burrill, 1997) to describe this gathering. These small groups function for training and support of outreach. White (1902) describes small groups as a requirement of every church:

> The formation of small companies as a basis of Christian effort has been presented to me by One who cannot err. If there is a large number in the church, let the members be formed into small companies, to work not only for the church members, but for unbelievers. If in one place there are only two or three who know the truth, let them form themselves into a band of workers. (pp. 21, 22)

These groups are specifically mentioned as being for the purpose of reaching unbelievers.

Ellen White wrote much about methods of evangelism. Several books that she wrote, and many more that have been compiled from her writings, focus on telling others about Jesus. White (1915) wrote that when involved in proclamation ministry, Christ must be uplifted above all else. All doctrines of the church must reflect the truth of the crucifixion.

A large amount of Ellen White's written material focuses on the church and its members transforming lives in each community by meeting needs. White describes meeting health needs, caring for the hungry and poor, and taking care of children. In *Ministry of Healing* (1905), she describes Christ's method of reaching the world:

> Christ's method alone will give true success in reaching the people. The Saviour mingled with men as one who desired their good. He showed His sympathy for them,

ministered to their needs, and won their confidence. Then He bade them, "Follow Me." (p. 143)

The Proclamational aspect of inviting people to follow Jesus comes only after four steps of interaction with people and meeting community needs.

This passage goes on to indicate that we should spend more time in transformational outreach than in the sermonic proclamation of the message of Christ. Living out the love of Jesus, not just talking about it should be a primary focus of the Christian. But that does not exclude the importance of the spoken Word. Jesus' ministry was not complete without the invitation and challenge being given to "follow." Ellen White repeatedly emphasized the importance of all believers, including young people, being involved in outreach. She taught that small groups should gather together for encouragement and training for outreach. These groups could work together to minister to the local community. As Christians, gathered in small groups, worked for those around them, they could participate in meeting felt needs of neighbors. As the church exhibits and shows the practical love of Jesus, opportunities will arise to proclaim the truths of Scripture and to give invitations to follow Jesus and begin to serve Him.

Summary and Implications of Literary Findings

The above works in no way represent an exhaustive view of material related to this topic of Millennials. Due to limitations of time and space, the literature reviewed is limited to issues that relate most directly to the scope of this study—the proposal of a training methodology to involve Millennials in transformational community outreach. Studies on the Millennial Generation look at positive characteristics and challenges of church involvement. Professional works on philosophies of missional outreach reveal a need for churches and members to be involved beyond the walls of the church. Studies look at methodologies for discovering the needs in a community. Practical works look at reasons and methods for training Millennials for outreach.

Millennial generation studies reveal that Millennials are the biggest and most diverse generation. They tend to be very teachable and desire working in learning groups. They desire to make a difference in the world, but the younger portion of this generation is faced with the experience of overprotection resulting in the lack of skills to carry projects through to completion. The church has mistakenly generated the philosophy of Moralistic Therapeutic Deism, which basically says that whatever one thinks is fine, as long as it makes the person happy and good. Many Millennials are positive about living a spiritual life, but are unsure of the institution of the church.

Studies in outreach philosophies indicate continued movements toward being "missional" having an outward looking focus. Churches need to think and act beyond the walls of the church, and need to be an active force for good in the community. Studies recognize that sodality and modality models can work together by being a part of the community as well as gathering for worship and inspiration. An important part of outreach focus must continue to be the proclamation of the gospel, partnered with acts of love and service.

Works that look at community development investigate methods for discovering the needs in the community and strengths of the church and bringing those together. This does involve research such as demographics, but also depends on the building of community relationships. This is done by interviewing leaders, talking to individuals, and observing the neighborhood. This is not a quick, short-term event, but something that develops as time and energy are put to use.

Studies show the importance of getting Millennials trained for outreach. Millennials that are involved in active service for others are more likely to be engaged spiritually in the life of the church. This generation also has a desire to be involved in projects that make a difference in the community and in the world. Nothing can make a more satisfying difference than impacting someone with the gospel. Because Millennials often prefer working in groups and are seeking for places of community, small groups are a natural way for young people to be trained and to find places to serve. This generation is also often seeking for mentors, so this provides an opportunity for different age groups to work together to make a difference for God.

Instructions for the Seventh-day Adventist Church in several of these areas are also emphasized in the writings of Ellen White.

As seen through a survey of these literary works, a model for Transformational Community Outreach by Millennials involves a three-fold process. First, small groups of young people and mentors must be formed for study, fellowship, training, and reflection. Second, community needs must be assessed by interviews and observation. Third, small groups must be encouraged and guided into action to meet the community needs using the collective gifts of the group and church. The three parts of this process form the training and curriculum for Chapter 4.

CHAPTER 4

A METHODOLGY AND IMPLEMENTATION OF
OUTREACH-ORIENTED SMALL GROUPS

Introduction

The Christian life is truly one of action. This action is a growth process that takes a new Christian from initially believing in God and accepting Jesus as Lord of their life to participating in acts of sharing the gospel with others and serving the world around them. Preparation for, and participation in, this growth process is greatly aided by being part of a vibrant community of believers. This chapter explores a plan to help disciples, particularly high school students, move through the process of *Knowing*, *Growing*, and *Going*. This will be partially accomplished by experiencing fellowship in a small group setting of faith that will help to provide training and opportunities to be involved in outreach.

From the first day of Jesus' public ministry, He called disciples to follow Him and to be with Him. These disciples left their careers and plans, they spent time with Jesus, and they acknowledged Him as Savior (John 1:39; Matt 4:19; 16:16, Mark 3:14; Luke 5:27). They knew Jesus personally, and spent around three years experiencing a close relationship with Him.

These disciples left all to be with Jesus, and their experience with Jesus was a time of continual learning. They observed the ministry of Jesus and were taught what it meant to participate in that ministry. They were trained in service, prayer, and preaching through instruction, stories, and reflection (Matt 5:1; 13:36; Mark 6:31; 9:29; Luke 11:1).

Jesus did more than just spend time with His disciples and tell them about ministry. He actually involved them in active ministry. Even while Jesus remained on earth, He sent the disciples out to go and preach, teach, and heal. The 12 were sent out two by two. They were sent out again with the 70 as others were trained and equipped (Mark 3:14; Luke 9:2; 10:1).

It was in the Great Commission, shared by Jesus before he returned to heaven (Matt 28:16-20), that the process of discipleship was to be an ongoing plan. The disciples were told to make disciples, helping people to know who Jesus was and what He had done. They were to baptize and teach, helping new Christians to grow in their faith. And finally, inherent in the Great Commission itself, these new believers were to be witnesses of Jesus in all the world (Acts 1:8; 8:4).

As the disciples began their ministry, they continued to follow through with this plan. This is seen clearly in the opening verses of 1 John. John writes that he, along with the other apostles, had "seen" Jesus, and "bear witness" to what they had heard and experienced. They were passing along the lessons and truth that they had learned so that the new Christians could have "fellowship" with both Jesus and the church, the Body of Christ (1 John 1:1-4). This was proven to be an effective means of discipleship and evangelism as seen in the rapid spread of the early Christian church (Acts 2:41; 5:14; 8:4; 9:31).

Unfortunately, it seems that many Christians today have not been actively engaged in this process of Christian growth. As Kidder indicates, "The vast majority of our members are not engaged in any form of witnessing" (2011, p. 129). They have forgotten the Great Commission, they have failed to be Salt and Light to the world around them (Matt 5:13-16), they have not grasped their role in the "priesthood of all believers" (1 Pet 2:9), and they have not utilized the power of the Holy Spirit to be witnesses from their own neighborhood to the ends of the earth (Acts 1:8).

It is only as Christians are fully engaged in each facet of the Christian life that they can live their lives as committed disciples. These facets of *knowing*, *growing*, and *going* are laid out in the ministry of Jesus and the apostles. This discipleship process will be explored through the ministry context of the Georgia-Cumberland Academy Church, an examination of successful small group strategies, and the development of a small group-based community outreach plan.

The Setting for Ministry

The Georgia-Cumberland Academy Church worships on the campus of Georgia-Cumberland Academy (GCA) at 351 Academy Drive, Calhoun, GA. This campus sits in the beautiful hills of northwest Georgia on the banks of the Oostanala River. The church, the academy, and Coble Elementary School share the 550-acre campus. The GCA Church, with a current membership of about 280, worships in the David C. Cress Youth Worship Center. This 550-seat sanctuary was completed in 2005.

The GCA Church is part of the Georgia-Cumberland Conference of Seventh-day Adventists with headquarters also in Calhoun, Georgia. The Georgia-Cumberland Conference is made up of 38,960 members, 166 churches, 35 schools, and employs 136 pastors (Office of Archives, Statistics, and Research, 2015).

This church was founded in 1993 by a group of members from the Calhoun Seventh-day Adventist Church who felt a full-time church was needed on the academy campus. While the academy first opened its doors for education in 1965, the property itself has a long connection with the Adventist Church. After seeking advice from Ellen White in 1908, Emeline Hurlbutt bought property in Reeves, Georgia, for the purpose of creating a sanitarium, training school, and farm. In the early 1960s, the Georgia-Cumberland Conference bought the land from the Layman's Foundation and begun constructing buildings for a boarding academy (Georgia-Cumberland Academy, 2016).

The ministry of the church and school are closely intertwined. While the church has about 280 members, it also ministers to approximately 250 students, with about 190 residing in on-campus dormitories. When school is in session, the average attendance is about 325, but during summer breaks church attendance is around 110.

The church membership has grown steadily in the last several years. From 2003 to 2016, church membership has more than doubled from 129 to 282 (Georgia-Cumberland Academy Church, 2016a). See Figure 1 for more details. The growth accelerated after the new church facility opened in 2005. Prior to the current sanctuary building, worship services took place in the academy chapel, which seats just over 250 people. When students were present, there was not much room for church members and visitors.

Most of this church growth was biological growth, primarily through the baptism of church members' children (joined sometimes by academy students), and transfer growth as families moved into the area for the Adventist education opportunities (Georgia-Cumberland Academy Church, 2016a). While the church has seen a steady growth rate, the baptisms have remained at the same rate. This lack of evangelistic "kingdom" growth is one of the challenges this project attempts to address (J. White, 2014).

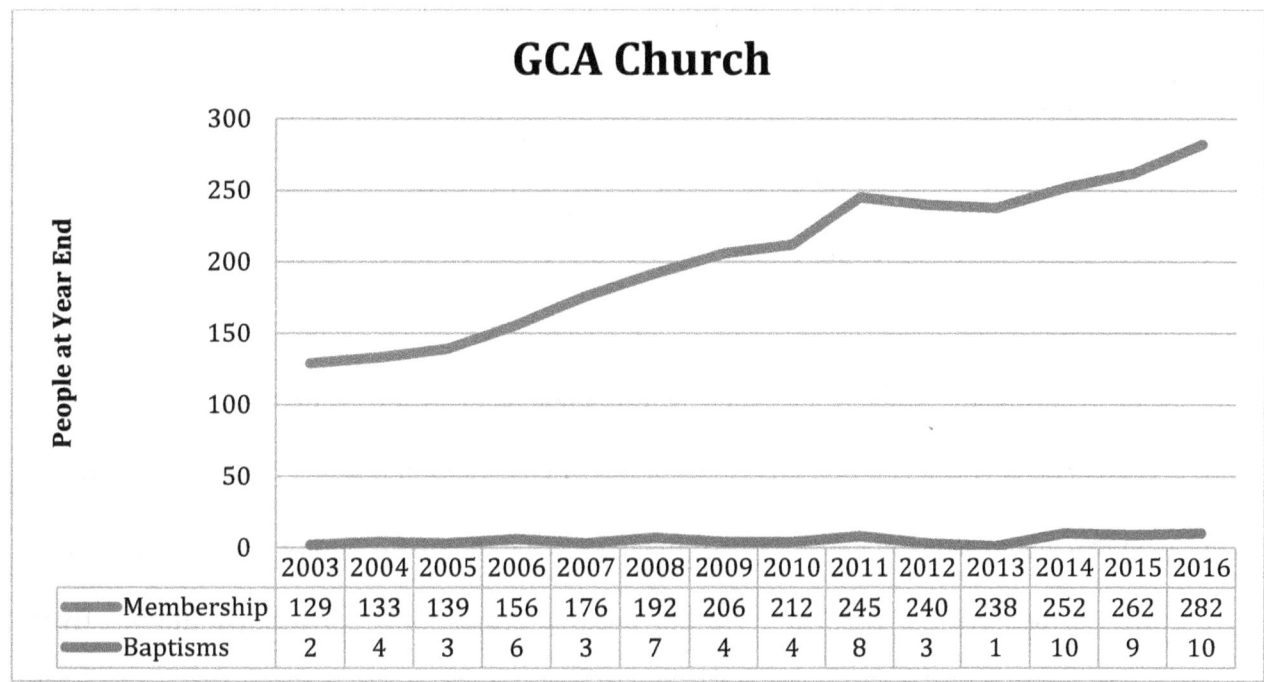

Figure 1. The membership and baptisms of the GCA Church (2003-2016). This figure examines the total membership and the yearly baptisms of the GCA Church.

From Captured Hearts to Developed Disciples

For about 15 years, the GCA Church has had a mission statement that reads, "The GCA Church Family exists to capture the hearts and minds of young people and to develop them into fully devoted disciples of Jesus Christ" (Georgia-Cumberland Academy Church, 2016b). For many years, GCA students have been deeply involved in the church on every level, from teaching in children's Sabbath School and serving as greeters, to leading worship praise groups and serving on church board and committees.

The primary focus of the church had been solely on the academy students, allowing other churches to focus on reaching the community.

As seemingly effective as this approach has been, it began to be apparent that some element of ministry was missing. One thing that is easily noticed is the lack of "kingdom" church growth as noted above. Even though the students were hopefully being developed into "fully-devoted disciples of Jesus," they were not having the opportunity to see the Great Commission being fulfilled in their church. If students were not seeing the gospel being shared, then they were not likely to grow to share it themselves.

Another challenge was noted through conversations and interactions with former students and alumni. While no direct survey of GCA alumni has been taken, anecdotal evidence and personal interaction seems to indicate that many former GCA students are turning their backs on the church as they move through life into young adulthood. Even with the emphasis on church involvement in academy, many of these students are drifting away during their college years. Kinnaman and Hawkins (2011) indicate that vast numbers of Millennials are leaving the church, with some estimates around 60%. It did not seem that the story was any better among GCA alumni. Something was wrong.

At GCA, it seems as if students were often looked at primarily as only "targets" of evangelism that need more knowledge about God. They were not being considered as potential "sharers" of the gospel. Many of these students have grown up in the church, know the doctrines, and have made multiple decisions to follow God. But they have not been inspired, trained, or equipped to act as a disciple maker.

The Great Commission was given to all disciples. Disciples are supposed to go and make more disciples (Burrill, 1996). Christians are supposed to let their light shine (Matt 5:16), young people were told to "preach the Word" (2 Tim 4:2). One element that seemed to be missing in the church's strategic plan was the active engagement of young people in sharing their faith with others.

With this challenge in mind, a strategy was designed to move students from accepting Jesus as their Lord and Savior to joining in community outreach and ministry as disciple-makers through participation in outreach-oriented small groups.

As Jesus was about to return to heaven, He left a Great Commission to His followers. This commission was to go, to make disciples, to baptize, and to teach (Matt 28:19, 20). Jesus makes it clear that for the church to be healthy today, each of these elements is needed. It is not enough for a new believer to be baptized. They must grow into a disciple. By definition and example, a disciple will also be involved in the process of developing new disciples. The Great Commission remains unfulfilled if Christians are not actively making disciples.

The first disciples of Jesus took this plan to heart. They knew Jesus, they had grown in their understanding of his message and mission, and then the time came to go to the world. After weeks of waiting and praying, this commission of Jesus was mightily enacted on the day of Pentecost (Acts 2). After 3,000 people were baptized, in their effort to make disciples and to teach as instructed by Jesus, the apostles met with small groups of believers in their homes. These groups contained four key elements: the apostles' teaching, fellowship, breaking bread, and prayer (Acts 2:42).

And so the cycle started again. As new disciples *KNOW* about the message of Jesus, they *GROW* in their knowledge and involvement, and then are ready to *GO* and make new disciples.

This biblical process became the basis for the Discipleship Strategy at the Georgia-Cumberland Academy Church.

Know, Grow, Go

The GCA Church Mission statement mentioned above explained why the GCA Church exists on the academy campus. Elders, board members, and leaders began to explore another question, "What do we need to do to make sure that mission is fulfilled?" With prayer, study, and discussion, a discipleship strategy was formed. In order to fulfill the mission of the church, students (and members) must be lead through the process to *Know*, *Grow*, and *Go*.

First, students must be given opportunity to *know* Jesus. The GCA Church seeks to "capture the hearts and minds through inspiring worships, small groups, and by encouraging personal devotional life" (GCA Church, 2016b).

As students come to know God, the next step is for them to *grow* in their faith and walk with God. The church desires to help students "develop skills in church-based ministries and leadership through training, experience, small groups, and mentorships" (GCA Church, 2016b).

The final step is for students to be trained and encouraged to *go* by "sending fully devoted disciples to share the everlasting gospel through community service, and personal, public, and global outreach" (GCA Church, 2016b).

Each part of this Discipleship Plan incorporates a segment of the long-term mission statement, but it also gives the church a blueprint for fulfilling this mission.

The Basic7 Plan

To give even more direction and accountability to the Discipleship Strategy, a Strategic Action Plan was developed. This plan has been adapted from the Army of Youth Program (Serns, 2015). The Strategic Action Plan seeks to give concrete, measureable actions that church members and students can participate in to move through the discipleship process.

This plan, known as Basic7, involves seven activities that are considered essential to the Christian life (Georgia-Cumberland Academy Church, 2016b). Students are encouraged to participate in these activities during their time in high school. These seven items are:

1. Engage in daily Bible study and prayer for six months
2. Participate in a small group
3. Experience three church ministries
4. Participate in three church leadership internships
5. Win someone to Jesus and the Adventist Movement
6. Help start Adventist work in a new area or be involved in public sharing of the Three Angels Message
7. Go on a mission trip

The first two activities on this list are for the purpose of helping participants to *Know* Jesus more through personal and community Bible study and fellowship. Items 2 through 4 are designed to help students *Grow* in skill and desire in a variety of ministry opportunities. Finally, items 5 through 7 are to encourage participants to *Go* as they will be involved in personal, public, and global outreach.

This list of seven items is in no way exhaustive of what it means to live an active Christian life, but it is believed that as a student (or any other church member) participates in these ministry fundamentals, their life will be moving in a positive direction, and they will likely be strengthening their spiritual walk. Just as the Great Commission was given to some disciples still in doubt (Matt 28:17), people will see their faith grow as they engage in these actions of discipleship.

This process is not linear. Doubting disciples were asked to fulfill the Gospel Commission and did so boldly. One does not have to move through this process in a step-by-step manner, and most people will likely be developing in most of the areas at the same time. One may enter into the discipleship process at any step, but to truly be a fully-devoted disciple, growth in all areas will be taking place.

This list also is designed to hold the church body accountable. "Church involvement seems to be a function of opportunity, leadership support and peer influence" (Barna Group, 2013b, p. 7). The Church must look at its variety of ministry opportunities and make sure that each one is helping to provide one of the Basic7 elements to help students to *Know*, *Grow*, or *Go*.

Due to the time limitations in the scope of this project, it is impossible to adequately develop each of these seven areas. So in light of the ongoing challenges of developing fully devoted disciples, while the church is implementing the Basic7 elements, this project seeks to concentrate on just one portion of the plan, to develop small groups for the purpose of promoting community outreach. This will serve as a bridge between *Know* and *Go*.

Exploring a Process for Outreach-Oriented Small Groups

As summarized in the last chapter, a survey of current literature revealed a three-fold process for creating a model of small groups for Transformational Community Outreach by young people. This process included: (a) small groups for fellowship and training, (b) an assessment of community needs through interviews and observation, and (c) guiding small groups into action in meeting community needs. These three elements are further explored in the next section.

Small Groups for Fellowship and Training

As seen in a previous chapter, small groups are a part of the biblical model in both the Old and New Testaments. Moses, Jesus, and the disciples gathered people into small groups for organization, for fellowship, and for instruction. The best description of what these groups looked like in the New Testament is found in Acts 2:42, "And they continued steadfastly in the apostles' doctrine and fellowship, in the breaking of bread, and in prayers." Fellowship is one of the four key elements of small groups as seen in this passage. These small gatherings of Christian believers had a distinct role in the rapid growth of the early church.

Many Christians today only experience ministry-related activities for an hour or two at church each week. They are missing out on the growth and community that takes place from gathering together with other believers. John remembers the close and intimate fellowship that the disciples had with Jesus (1 John 1:1-4). The gospel stories relate how the time Jesus spent with his disciples included instruction, praise and rebuke, and rest and relaxation (Matt 5:1; 16:17; Luke 9:10; 9:55).

Assessing Community Needs

As Jesus entered new territory, he became aware of peoples' needs in various ways. Jesus sometimes approached those with obvious needs and offered his help. Often times people came to Him asking for help (Mark 2:4; Luke 8:41; John 2:3), still other times Jesus asked questions about what was needed (John 4:7), and sought out those in need (5:6; 9:7). Similar actions were seen in the early church. They healed those who had need (Acts 3:6; 16:18; 28:8) and they met physical needs when requests were received (4:34; 6:3; 9:36). Sometimes the apostles observed the city to see what needs might be present and how they could be met (Acts 17:23).

Service-Oriented Outreach

As the early church met together in homes and small groups, they were also active in caring for those in need. With Jesus, they had participated in the ministries of teaching, preaching, and healing (Matt 4:23; 9:35). These activities are also seen in the book of Acts. They cared for those in material need (Acts 2:45; 4:34; 6:3) as well as those with physical and health needs (Acts 3:6; 9:34; 20:10). It seems the disciples had taken to heart the instruction of Jesus to treat every person in the same way they would treat Jesus Himself (Matt 25:40).

Serving others helps each Christian take the focus off of self and put it on other people in need. Service helps individuals to look for needs in the world around them, and to utilize their spiritual gifts to meet the needs of others as one is able (Keller, 1989). Projects that serve a community cause can also be a way to reach the "nones," those who are indifferent towards God and religion (J. White, 2014).

Exploring Successful Small Group Strategies

Ellen White, one of the founders of the Seventh-day Adventist Church, notes the importance of small groups focused on outreach.

> The formation of small companies as a basis of Christian effort has been presented to me by One who cannot err. If there is a large number in the church, let the members be formed into small companies, to work not only for the church members, but for unbelievers. (1902, pp. 21, 22)

This idea serves as a basis for developing a small group strategy.

Several churches are currently involved in successful strategies for small groups engaged in community outreach. Two of these churches were studied to learn key elements of success. For outlines of these interviews see Appendix A.

In addition, one book, *Activate* by Nelson Searcy (2008), was closely studied due to the successful adaptation of its strategy by several churches, including one of the churches studied.

Church 1: Richardson, Texas, Seventh-day Adventist Church, Dan Serns, Senior Pastor

Small groups are a vital element of the Richardson Church. "Everyone is better off in in a group or a number of groups" (D. Serns, personal communication, December 4, 2015). Groups take various forms and shapes, but they each have a goal or challenge to bring someone to Jesus in the course of a year. To form a group, one needs a collection of three leaders: (a) Up Reach leader to direct the group toward God, (b) In Reach leader to connect the group to each other, and (c) Outreach leader to help the group in working to bring someone to Jesus. Each group also needs a church board mentor to listen, advise, and represent on the church board.

The church seeks to have the number of groups be equivalent to 10% of church attendance. With a church attendance of about 650 people, their goal is to have about 65 small groups in action. At the end of each eight-week group session, there is a church-wide reaping series that allows opportunities for interested group members to take a stand for Jesus.

Several key insights were gained from the interview with Serns. First, it is expected that church leadership will take part in the group strategy, either leading a group or mentoring group leaders. Second, their strategy involves groups being a part of every facet of the church from Sabbath School and the Pathfinder Club, to the young adult group and the choir. Finally, all groups are challenged to work to bring someone to accept Jesus and be baptized. There are several Reaping Event opportunities throughout the year to provide natural invitations for this to take place.

Church 2: Pioneer Memorial Church, Berrien Springs, Michigan, Rodlie Ortiz, Pastor for Outreach/Evangelism

Pioneer Memorial Church (PMC) started to use the small group strategy from *Activate* (Searcy, 2008) in 2012. Their overall church discipleship strategy is *Connect, Serve, Grow, Go*. Small groups, called GROWgroups are a "core piece of discipleship delivery" (R. Ortiz, personal communication, December 10, 2015). These groups are affinity groups, meeting for just a semester. Because this church is located on a university campus, promotion and groups begin shortly after the academic semester begins. Group outreach is an important element for this group strategy. Each group selects its own outreach project.

The interview with Ortiz yielded several more insights for a small group strategy. First is the importance of pastoral leadership. The pastor is key to promotion and the ongoing success of this strategy. Pastors should lead by example by leading (or at least joining) a group. This includes pastoral leadership and promotion of the group process. Another insight is the importance of continuing accountability, encouragement, and follow-up with group leaders as the GROWgroup semester goes on. A final insight is the need in an academic setting to make sure group strategy fits into the school calendar. This includes the time frame for beginning the groups, as well as anticipating less group participation during the summer months.

Activate, by Nelson Searcy (2008)

This book has a different small group philosophy than many other books. One of the key elements that stand out is the call for groups of a larger size (20 members, instead of 10-12). With more people, it is often easier to make friends, and less likely to have a "non-talking group." It also has a basic goal of group members using the group to discover and build friendships, not deep, intimate bonds. Many people, especially men, are less likely to share their inner feelings with more than two or three people; therefore, that expectation can challenge the group attitude. While many small group ideas are based on long-term small groups with no definite ending time, these groups are short-term by design, lasting about 12 weeks, with a new trimester of groups beginning every four months. There is a month of promotion and planning, followed by the three-month group process. These groups are designed for groups to serve together in an outreach project as part of the group experience. Another important principle is that the senior pastor must be a champion of the small group process. These groups become a place to find the next-generation of leaders as people are mentored in the leadership process during group time. Many new leaders are then ready to take a group leadership role during a future trimester.

Implementation of a Strategy for Outreach-Oriented Small Groups

Based on a study of the Bible, the reading of pertinent current literature, and the examination of successful small group strategies in other churches, a strategy was created to develop a small group ministry that would encourage and train members and students to be involved in community outreach. This would involve a three-part process. The first step would be to establish small group communities at the GCA Church for fellowship, as well as encouragement and training for outreach. Next, community needs would be assessed through interviews and observation. Finally, group leaders and participants would be encouraged and trained to meet community needs.

Evaluation of this project would be primarily through anonymous student surveys. This would gauge student participation and growth in several discipleship areas (Thayer, 2004), including attitude toward community outreach. Surveys would be given both before and after the project to note any changes in outreach participation and attitudes in those that took part in the small group process. These surveys may be seen in Appendix B.

Small Group Foundation

Small groups had not been a part of the culture at the GCA Church. Beginning in August 2014, a strategy of affinity-based GROWgroups was introduced to the ministries of the GCA Church. These groups focused on a variety of differing topics and interests. Following a period of promotion, GROWgroups would meet for a group semester of about eight weeks, after which a new cycle with new groups would begin for the next semester. These groups are for the purpose of building community around a common interest while at the same time providing avenues to encourage community outreach.

These GROWgroups continued during each academic semester: Fall 2014, Spring 2015, Fall 2015, Spring 2016, and will continue in the future. The rest of this ministry project builds on the foundation of these small groups.

Evaluating Community Needs

To discover and evaluate felt needs in the Calhoun area, several community leaders were interviewed. Leaders were selected that assist in a variety of services in the Calhoun community. These leaders were asked their opinion on what were the greatest needs in the community, and how the GCA Church and students could possibly assist with meeting those needs. Four different leaders were interviewed from a variety of community organizations including the Voluntary Action Center, CREATION Health, the United Way, and the Imagination Station. See Appendix C for interview questions and outlines.

The needs that were mentioned by community leaders fell into four main categories. The first area of great need is financial assistance, especially for health-care related needs, but also for things like household bills and food. A second area of need is that of health education and lifestyle training. Many do not know about the basic points for healthy living, or do not care to make lifestyle changes until major health issues arise. Another area of need is in the area of youth mentoring and tutoring. There are many young people who do not have positive role models from parents or older siblings. This impacts both the decision-making process and the success in academics. A final area frequently mentioned is that of basic home assistance for the elderly. This includes both things like cleaning and home and lawn maintenance.

Project Groups

Building on the GROWgroup foundation, this project focused on developing a process for the creation of small groups with a community outreach focus. This two-part process consists of a six-week *Group Leader Training Series* and a five-week *Reach the World* Small Group Curriculum. These two units can be used for successive training, but can also stand alone as complimentary learning events.

Group Leader Training Series

The *Group Leader Training Series* consists of six sessions that are primarily shared through online video presentations. The first five sessions are video sessions averaging about ten minutes. Participants receive one video a week via e-mail to watch on their own schedule and then respond to reflection questions via e-mail. The sixth session is a gathering of all participants for final training, questions, and encouragement for future leadership. The online format seeks to accommodate the busy schedule and technological usage of the academy students by "flipping the classroom," allowing them to view the instructional material on their own time, while still providing opportunity for questions and reflection (Bergmann & Sams, 2012; Morris, 2015; Rideout, 2015).

The target audience was any GCA student that was interested in involvement and potential leadership in this small group ministry. Therefore, the participants were diverse in race, gender, and spiritual maturity, but were all high school students. This training process was introduced to the Junior and Senior classes during Bible class, and students were invited to voluntarily participate. Initially there were 20 students that expressed interest, while 10 followed through and completed the group training.

The video sessions ranged from six to 12 minutes. Each session covered a topic related to GROWgroup fundamentals and leadership. These instructional sessions included scripture, teachings of Ellen White and contemporary writers, as well as some video clips. Each session ended with two reflection questions for the participant to respond to via e-mail. The purpose of these sessions was to engage in the discipleship process to *Know, Grow,* and *Go* through training and leadership in future small groups. Topics for these sessions can be seen in Table 1.

Date Sent	Session	Description	Time
11/12/2015	Introduction	A look at how this video series will work	2:20
11/23/2015	1) Elements of Small Group	Reviews key group elements from Acts 2:42—Bible, fellowship, food, prayer	6:36
12/1/2015	2) Fellowship	Examines the importance of community in a small group	11:08
12/8/2015	3) GROWgroup	Specifics of the GROWgroup ministry philosophy	12:23
12/16/2015	4) Outreach	Explores how groups can fulfill "Christ's Method Alone"	9:52
12/28/2015	5) Group Leadership	Examines key qualities for a group leader: prayer, caring, communication	8:49
1/13/2015	6) Gathering	Gathers all participants for review, reflection, questions, and planning	1 hour

Table 1. Dates, topics, and information for video sessions.

The video sessions were sent out once a week beginning in mid-November 2015 through December 2015, with Session 6 taking place in January 2016 with eight participants. At this final session, participants were encouraged to begin (or at least join) a GROWgroup with an outreach focus.

From this initial group, four went on to lead or co-lead a GROWgroup during Spring 2016. Evaluation of this video series was through group discussion at the final session, as well as follow-up conversations.

Reach the World Small Group Curriculum

The second aspect of this strategy was the creation a small group curriculum that focused primarily on the Christian's call to fulfill the Gospel Commission.

Again, the target audience was any student or church member that wanted to be involved in this small group ministry. Therefore the participants were diverse in race, gender, and spiritual maturity, but were primarily high school students. All students and church members were encouraged to participate through announcements and e-mail invitations. Also, those that completed the *Group Leader Training Series* were especially encouraged to take part in this group.

The *Reach the World* group curriculum looks at the biblical mandate for Christians to be involved in evangelism and outreach. Each group session begins with two icebreaker questions (Launch), reads a Bible passage (Call to Action), and explores that passage (Reflection). This is followed by a story from church history or contemporary life of someone taking part in outreach (Life in Action). The final two sections challenge participants to begin to think what an outreach project might look like for the group (Group Action) and individual (My Action). The topic of each group lesson can be seen in Table 2. Sample lessons may be seen in Appendix D.

This GROWgroup option was offered in January and February 2016, with a small group of five people participating. Of this group, three also participated in a newly formed Armuchee Community Outreach, along with many other students.

Title	Theme	Passage	Story	Personal Task
The Commission	Great Commission	Matt 28:16-20	Hudson Taylor	Learn family spiritual heritage
Power to Witness	Holy Spirit	Acts 1:4-8	Asbury Revival	List Sphere of Influence
Harvest in Great	Everyone Is Needed	Matt 9:35-38	D. T. Bourdeau	Discover gifts/skills
Share Your Story	Personal Testimony	Luke 8:35-39	Multiple Testimonies	Learn to share testimony
Christ's Method Alone	Compassion Evangelism	Matt 25:24-40	Anna Knight	Decide on outreach project

Table 2. Topics and theme of each lesson of *Reach the World* Curriculum.

Conclusion and Implications

In conclusion, based on a study of the Bible, the reading of pertinent current literature, and examining successful small group strategies in other churches, a small group strategy for community outreach was developed that included the creation of small groups for fellowship, the assessment of community felt needs, and guiding small groups to participate in community outreach.

In summary, this small group strategy will:

1. Create small groups where participants can experience Bible study, prayer, community, and training in a group sharing common interests.

2. Provide training, support, and encouragement for individuals to be involved in meeting felt needs in the community and to participate in the fulfilling the Gospel Commission.

3. Engage the community through interaction with community leaders for assessment and observation of felt needs.

4. Develop leaders and leadership skills as more individuals are encouraged and trained for leadership through small group opportunities.

5. Encourage integration of generations and different segments of the church body (members, staff, and students) through group and outreach participation.

The ultimate goal of this project is to see students fully engaged in the action-filled Christian life. As they move through the discipleship strategy (*Know*, *Grow*, and *Go*), students will be engaged in the fellowship of a small group, that together will be working to meet the felt needs of the community. As students grow in their Christian walk through small groups and community outreach, they will be actively involved in fulfilling the Gospel Commission, and will be developing into disciple-making Christians!

CHAPTER 5

OUTCOMES AND EVALUATIONS

Introduction

As evidenced in the ministry of Jesus and His disciples in the spirit-led early church, community and service have always been two key elements in the Christian life. These elements continue to remain important to gatherings of believers in our current day. Living in community helps to bond followers of Christ together in their commitment to Jesus and to each other, while living a live of service connects believers with the world around them as they seek to fulfill the Great Commission. This study has sought a connection of these two facets of the Christian experience.

This project has reached a point of completion, but many potential areas of study and learning remain. While it has been discovered that students feel that involvement in small groups helps to equip them for outreach, there are many other areas of interest that still need to be studied in further detail. Some of these areas include: the optimal group format for both discipleship and participation, the impact of cross-generational groups, the most effective means of engaging groups in community outreach, and the changing characteristics of future generations.

Each of these study areas mentioned will be examined in this chapter, along with a review of the process for developing small groups for outreach, important keys that have been learned, an examination of survey results indicating life changes, as well as a personal journey of a church leader in this group development process.

Summary of Project

The foundation for this project consisted of a development of a small group strategy for community outreach. The purpose of this project was to create a growing, vibrant, church-wide, small group ministry that would be an ongoing part of the church life and would be an integral part of equipping participants for community outreach.

The target audience for this study included any student at GCA that wanted to grow in their walk with God and in community with other students and church members. The participants in these activities were very diverse. They were primarily GCA students, but also included members of the GCA Church, and therefore were diverse in age, race, and gender. They also had a spiritual diversity that ranged from long-term church members, to teenagers active and inactive in their faith. A few were non-religious international students that are still learning about Christianity.

Over two school years, a church-wide small group program was implemented in a church that previously had no small group emphasis. After evaluating various small group approaches, it was decided that an affinity-based small groups model would be utilized, allowing church members and students to build community around common interests. These groups, in this context called GROWgroups, were encouraged to participate in community outreach as a unit.

Group leaders were trained, students and church members were recruited to take part, small groups were formed, community needs were assessed, and outreach projects were developed. Students were surveyed before and after the formation of the

GROWgroups. Through these surveys, it could be seen that students who participated in the GROWgroup process felt that the these groups were beneficial for their personal spiritual growth, and for outreach training and experience.

Individual GROWgroups functioned for a specific period of time during one semester. At the conclusion of one semester, some groups continued, while new groups also formed. This program was implemented and evaluated over the course of four academic semesters during two academic school years. For each GROWgroup semester, leaders were recruited and trained, and then groups were advertised to students and church members. Each semester, some groups were very successful, while others had a difficult time gaining members.

Some group leaders were involved in a video *Group Leader Training Series* curriculum. This five-part video curriculum explored the various aspects of group leadership in a format of self-study, and ended with a gathering for reflection and questions.

Community needs were assessed, and group leaders were encouraged to look for ways to serve as a group to help to meet these community needs. Outreach projects included community-service type projects, public evangelism, and friendship evangelism.

This project was done in one church location for a specified period of time, but much of the information and principles observed here could possibly be transferred to other churches and schools. It is hoped that this plan will be utilized in the future as the needs and contexts determine.

This strategy for small groups and community outreach was researched, planned, and implemented for the purpose of answering one question: Does participation in an affinity-based small group help inspire and equip a student for participation in community outreach? The answer seems to be affirmative.

But there are several other questions related to this project that remain unanswered. First, this project did not answer what format of small groups works best to get students equipped to reach out to their community. This project utilized affinity-based small groups, but other group formats may also be effective. Second, it did not achieve a high percentage of participation of students in the small groups and outreach projects. Different methods of recruiting and advertising could be done in different contexts to see what is most effective in achieving a high percentage of participation. Third, it did not fully discover what the best method for training leaders would be. This project utilized a video-based, self-study program with personal follow-up. Small-group based training, one-on-one training, or "on-the-job" training are some other options that could be utilized for future studies.

GROWgroups in Action

Year 1

After vision-casting and recruiting, small groups were formed. The initial semester of GROWgroups in Fall 2014 had seven groups with approximately 48 participants. The number of participants included students, church members, and guests. Some participants were in more than one group. Group leader training was in the form of a monthly individual check-in with the pastor for discussion, questions, and encouragement.

The second semester of groups was in Winter 2015. During this winter semester there were 10 groups with about 91 participants. These groups gathered regularly for their intended purpose, and were also encouraged to participate in outreach events as a group. This outreach did not always take place as a group. If unable to participate as a group, GROWgroup members were encouraged to take part in other planned outreach opportunities. These included ministry to children at the local Imagination Station and the Boys and Girls Club, as well as local food banks.

One group that focused primarily on outreach during the winter semester was a "Radical Teachings" Group. This group of seven students met regularly in preparation for presenting an outreach seminar, *The Radical Teachings of Jesus* (Morris, 2009), at the Calhoun Seventh-day Adventist Church in February. Many of these same students also did their evangelistic presentation during a seminar in Panama during the Spring Break mission trip resulting in four baptisms.

Year 2

In Fall 2015, during the second year of GROWgroups at GCA Church, there were 15 groups with 125 participants. Leadership training continued as one-on-one communication between the pastor and the group leader as well as through the *Group Leadership Video Training*. The Spring 2016 GROWgroup semester had 15 groups with 121 participants.

While all groups were encouraged to participate in some form of outreach as groups or as individuals, some groups focused specifically on outreach, including: *Bethlehem Live*, a group that gathered weekly to prepare for the church's Christmas outreach that included about 50 students; *Reach the World* Outreach Training; a *GO* group of about 30 students (involved in community outreach to nearby community of Armuchee, Georgia); and a *Touched by Jesus* group involving over 50 students that met regularly to produce a week-long drama outreach based on the final week of the life of Jesus.

The Small Group Process

As this affinity-based small group program was implemented, several key factors for successful small groups on an academy campus were revealed. These factors seem to be instrumental in the ongoing success of a small group ministry with an outreach orientation.

The first factor for small group success is to always include the key biblical elements of small groups. These are most clearly seen in Acts 2:42: "And they continued steadfastly in the apostles' doctrine and fellowship, in the breaking of bread, and in prayers." The key elements indicated here are: (a) Bible teaching, (b) fellowship, (c) sharing food, and (d) praying together. Including each of these keys in every group seemed to be instrumental in a successful small group strategy.

A gathering of Christians must be focused on the Bible and on bringing glory to God's name, even if the primary purpose of the gathering is not to study the Bible (1 Cor 10:31). People of all ages, but particularly youth and young adults, need more opportunities to build community with others who share common beliefs and interests (Carter, 2013). Food is a universal need, and sharing food together is a sign of welcoming hospitality and friendship (House, 2011, p. 188). And finally, as Christians pray together, they will grow in commitment to each other and to God (Wheeler, 2009, p. 15).

A second factor for successful small groups is in leadership development. The GROWgroup leaders need to receive basic training in how to lead a group, even though group leadership will be very different depending on the focus of each group. They must also receive ongoing support and communication as the group process continues to assist them in meeting any concerns or difficulties with in their groups (Searcy, 2008).

Perhaps most important in training leaders is an instillation of the vision of the GROWgroup process into the thinking of the group leaders. Group leaders must be challenged and reminded that they are part of something bigger, for a grand purpose of building lasting community in the church and reaching the needs of the neighborhood. Leaders must be reminded of the vision on an ongoing basis; particularly from semester to semester as new leaders are forming new groups. It is easy to just assume that everyone in the church is moving in the same direction, but continual vision casting and reminders are extremely vital.

A third factor in a successful outreach-oriented small group strategy is providing direction for outreach. In a boarding academy setting, most students are not familiar with the needs of the community and have little contact with the neighborhoods around the school. They do not know what potential outreach opportunities are there, so they must be advised and instructed. As community needs are assessed by church leadership and church members, GROWgroup leaders can be directed to outreach opportunities that will best meet the skills and talents of each particular group.

Initially, the GROWgroup project envisioned groups participating in outreach opportunities as a group. This idea was taught and encouraged, but it often did not end up happening in the expected way. As students have different schedules, and different gifts and talents, they also had interests in different types of outreach activity. Because of this, various types of outreach projects were developed and GROWgroup participants were encouraged to be involved both as groups and as individuals. This worked well for two reasons: (a) it allowed group members with different schedules and interests to still be engaged in outreach, and (b) it provided opportunities for students and church members that are not part of a GROWgroup to work along-side group members in fulfilling the Gospel Commission.

One example of this was the *GO* group to the nearby community of Armuchee. This group participated in Friendship Evangelism activities and community prayer about once a month. Participants included group members and leaders from other GROWgroups, as well as other students who were able to join in the outreach opportunities as they desired without being part of a group. Some of these student participants were not even professed Christians, yet were able to be involved in witnessing about Jesus.

A fourth factor for successful small groups in a boarding academy setting is allowing for flexibility for semesters, schedules, meetings, and other factors. Academy schedules are very busy, and students are less likely to join a group that will add to their stress levels and workloads. By allowing groups to change every semester, students recognize that their commitment is not "forever" and are more likely to get involved. At the same time, even with only semester long commitments, there are still times that students will miss meetings due to other obligations, study needs, and other factors. When these potential absences are anticipated in the process, groups are able to continue to function, even as an individual may not always be there. Students are not excluded from group participation and are still able to gain the benefit of community and outreach encouragement that they might otherwise miss out on by not having "time" to join a GROWgroup (Powell, Mulder, & Griffin, 2016, p. 188).

Finally, another significant contribution in small group success seemed to be based on the topics of individual groups. Anecdotally, the more directly related to outreach the GROWgroup topic was, seemingly the more commitment and sustainability was seen in the reaction of the group participants. While several groups of varied subject matters saw some success in the gathering of group members, groups that were more directly focused on outreach seemed to have commitments at a deeper level.

One example of this was the "Radical Teachings of Jesus" group (Morris, 2009). This group met several times over the course of a few months to plan and prepare for a short, public evangelistic meeting. These students spent time studying their topics from the Bible, learning their sermons, and praying for each other and the series. The commitment to the outreach project was greater when outreach was the main focus of the group. While this seems obvious, it is also shows the importance of sharing tangible outreach opportunities with groups as they are in the planning and formation stage.

In conclusion, some key factors required for developing a outreach-oriented small groups program are: a continuing focus on the biblical keys of a small group; a developed plan for training group leaders, including casting a vision for small groups; a method of discovering community needs and matching group and individual skills with those needs; flexibility in scheduling and attendance in groups; and helping groups form for a direct outreach purpose.

Analysis of Surveys

During each year of this project, students at GCA were given the opportunity to complete two separate surveys to note impact in participation in GROWgroup in a variety of spiritual indicators (see Appendix A). These surveys were primarily based on *The*

Christian Spiritual Participation Profile (J. Thayer, 1999). One survey was given at the beginning of each school year, and after two semesters of GROWgroups, the second was given at the conclusion of each year. The second survey of each year included several additional questions about participation and evaluation in the GROWgroup project. An analysis of these evaluative surveys indicated that students that participated in GROWgroups during a given school year found the GROWgroup program to be somewhat beneficial in several different areas, including personal spirituality, and in activities reflective of building community and involvement and training for service. These results will be discussed in the following sections.

Changes in Promotion

After year one, surveys and anecdotal conversations indicated that about 69% of students did not participate in GROWgroups, and some were not even aware of the GROWgroup vision or the continued existence of the groups. Despite promotional attempts, many were still unaware. Because of this awareness gap, promotion and recruitment was done with more intentionality for the second year of the GROWgroup process. Church and bulletin announcements were more prominent. Recruiting visits for group leaders was made at GCA Chapel and during Bible Class. After the second year group participation had risen slightly from 31% to 36% of the students (See Figure 2).

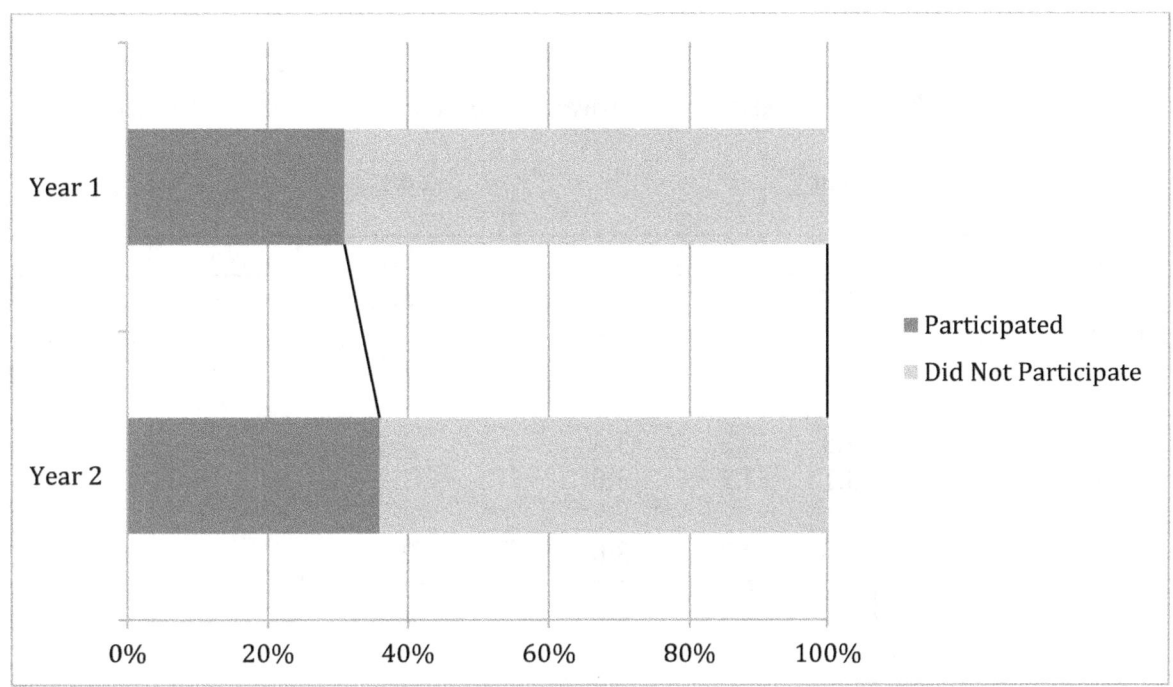

Figure 2. Percentage of GROWgroup participation among students, 2014-2016.

Benefits in Personal/Community Spirituality

Several survey questions looked at the students' frequency of Bible study and prayer, as well as participation in small groups with other believers. The post-survey results were sorted by those who participated in GROWgroups and those who did not.

After two years, the students that participated in GROWgroups self-scored higher in most of the survey categories, including Praying for Others, Helping Others, Meeting in a Small Group, and Serving in Ministry (see Table 3). This does not necessarily suggest causation, as it is possible that students that were willing to participate in GROWgroups previously exhibited these positive spiritual characteristics in their lives. The students that had participated in GROWgroups indicated that the one of biggest benefits of these groups was in the realm of their personal spiritual life.

Table 3

Survey Raw Data Results—Averages of Answers from Year 1 and Year 2 of Study

	Year 1			Year 2		
Question Summary	Pre	Post No	Post Yes	Pre	Post No	Post Yes
Pers. Spirituality	4.0	3.9	4.1	3.9	4.1	4.2
Outreach Exp.	3.2	3.1	3.4	3.2	3.3	3.2
Outreach Skills	3.1	3.0	3.5	3.1	3.0	3.2
Pray	3.3	3.2	3.3	3.3	3.2	3.3
Study Bible	3.1	2.7	3.0	3.1	3.0	3.2
Intro to Jesus	2.9	2.7	3.0	2.7	2.6	2.8
Assist in Teaching	3.2	3.1	3.7	3.0	3.1	3.3
Invite Unchurched	2.4	2.2	2.7	2.3	2.2	2.6
Praying for Others	3.6	3.3	3.7	3.4	3.2	3.5
Helping Others	3.7	3.2	3.8	3.2	3.1	3.4
Meet Small Group	2.9	2.8	3.5	2.7	2.7	3.1
Serve in Ministry	2.9	2.8	3.3	2.8	2.8	3.1
Rate Sp Health (10)	5.9	5.9	6.5	5.8	5.9	5.8
Participate in GG						
Evan Training			52%			59%
Active Outreach			33%			50%
Small Grp Interact			91%			97%
Emotional Benefit			6.2			5.0
Spiritual Benefit			6.3			5.4
Evangelism Benefit			5.1			4.6
Social Benefit			6.4			5.4

Note. Post No = GROWgroup non-participants; Post Yes = GROWgroup participants

Benefits in Community/Social Aspects

A second area of inquiry in the survey was participation in small groups and social activities. Again, the participants in GROWgroups did rate themselves slightly higher in these areas than those who did not participate in GROWgroups. Over 90% of participants felt that GROWgroups were most profitable in providing opportunity for participation in the community of the church. This was by far the highest-rated element of the GROWgroup survey. The participants noted a personal and group benefit to gathering together around a common interest.

Benefits in Service/Outreach Attitude

Survey questions also looked at characteristics relating to various areas of service to others and outreach. This includes questions on serving others in the community and in the church, inviting people to church, as well as evangelistic training and opportunity. GROWgroup participants rated themselves higher than non-participants in areas such as serving others, praying for others, and inviting non-members to church.

While GROWgroup participants found that this process benefitted them in the skills and attitudes towards evangelism and outreach, it did rate lower than both the spiritual and social aspects. Participants felt that GROWgroups were very adequate for evangelism training (59%), but fell short on providing opportunities for outreach and evangelism (Year 1—33%, Year 2—50%).

Potential Improvements

In a project of this scope, there are obviously in retrospect things that could have been done differently to bring about more of the desired results. These items could have allowed more people to engage in this process and be involved in sharing the gospel. When this project is used in the future, these items should be considered.

The first thing that could have improved the project would be to have included a smaller group that could have been tracked from beginning to end for changes in spiritual attitudes and involvement in outreach. This group could have been surveyed more specifically or even interviewed in a focus group setting. Interaction with this small cluster would have allowed for more direct reflection from students that were actively engaged in outreach or small groups.

Another change to this project procedure would have been to meet more regularly and strategically with group leaders. Particularly in the first year of the project, a better plan of leadership training and development would have set a more solid foundation for the ongoing success of the outreach-oriented small groups.

A final change that could have made this project better is to have developed a strategy for specifically recruiting participants in the outreach projects to join GROWgroups. Participants for GROWgroups were recruited at the beginning of each semester and outreach projects were developed for both group members and other individuals, but there was no mechanism to more immediately suggest to the individual outreach participants to become part of a GROWgroup. These individuals would have been welcomed to join a group at any time, but specific recruiting did not take place until the next semester.

These are just a few of the things in this project that could have been done differently that may have made the results more effective. It is suggested that when principles of this project as adapted to a future context, the elements be included.

Recommendations for Further Study

Because of limitations of time and scope, there are many areas that this project has not fully examined. Some of these unexplored areas would be beneficial for a more complete understanding of the small group process and its implementation of active community outreach among Millennials. This study has sought to develop a program of small groups in a local church, to assess community needs, and to encourage involvement in community outreach. The results of this study have shown that when individuals are active in Bible-based small groups and growing in community, they do feel better equipped to be involved in community outreach. Continued study and assessment of different forms of small groups and interaction with the community will be helpful to more fully develop a small group process that will best benefit both church members and the community.

Different Forms of Small Groups

This project implemented one form of a small group modeled from an aggregate of several different successful small group contexts. These affinity-based small groups were created to gather a group of people with a common interest to meet for a short period of time and to equip and engage the group members in community outreach. While the affinity-based model provides for many different group topics, including Bible study, exercise, cooking, sports, and other hobbies, it is noted that other models of small groups are also successfully practiced in many churches and may have similar results in encouraging participants to engage in outreach.

With the creation of a video-based *Group Leader Training Series*, it opens the possibility to other unconventional types of small groups that could resonate with those in the millennial generation and beyond. As long as the group model contains the biblical elements of small groups as provided in Acts 2:42 (biblical basis, fellowship, eating, prayer), what other models could be created?

In a world of technology, social media, and video-connected smart phones, would a virtual small group be possible, and could it still contain the biblical elements of a group? Could group members "fellowship" with one another, even if actual in-person contact is limited? These are just a few intriguing ideas that might prove beneficial to the spiritual growth of young people if studied and tested in the future.

Impact of Cross-Generational Groups

While this study focused primarily on the participation and training of students and young people, many of the GROWgroups at GCA Church also included older church members alongside students, and several of the groups were led by church members. While the impact of this cross-generational mingling was beyond the scope of this study, it seemed that the opportunity to spend time together is a benefit for both students and older members. People of difference ages are able to get to know one another, share with one another, and to serve together (Powell, Mulder, & Griffin, 2016).

Both age groups are able to contribute and each group is able to benefit from the other. Adults are able to instill wisdom and experience to the students, while the students can supply an energy and freshness to groups, to outreach, and to fellowship.

Different Methods of Outreach

Each community and each generation will have different forms of outreach that will work best to reach local community needs with both transformational and proclamational outreach. With changes in society, technology, and attitudes towards religion, different methods of outreach must be experimented with and explored. What are the best methods to reach those interacting on social media almost constantly? How can the church impact the growing number of individuals indifferent towards religion and the church? How can the stories of salvation enter the conversation of a society polarized to the extreme in matters as far reaching as politics and sports?

Transformational Community Outreach methods are often seen as a means to enter into someone's life, but ongoing ideas need to continue to also include strategies for proclamational sharing of the gospel of Jesus. Locations and methods will change but the community service opportunities must continue to pave the way for calls to follow the Savior.

Changes in Future Generations

The focus of this project was on the Millennial generation, those born between 1982 and 2002. This group was chosen because of the high school setting of this project. But in 2016, even before this project was fully completed, the younger students at GCA are no longer born in the years generally assigned to the Millennial Generation, but are now born in the transition period to the next generation.

It must be noted that any study that focuses on a particular age group or generation will soon find at least some of its information out of date and obsolete. This project researched broad characteristics of the Millennial generation. But the next generation, often referred to with a variety of names such as Gen Z, Builders, Founders, or Homeland generation (Seemiller & Grace, 2016), must also be researched to find the best methods of impacting their lives. Each generation must be studied anew to find its tendencies and norms. It is likely that much of the information related to small groups will carry over into future generations because a common need of humanity is to seek community and to desire a place of belonging. An old song states the need to have a place "where everybody knows your name" (Portnoy & Wurzback, 1982). This need will likely continue into future generations as well.

When any generation is studied, results only look at the broad picture. But generations are not just groups; they are made up of individual people. Each person, in each situation, will react differently and have different needs; therefore, interactions with each person will obviously vary. People need to be looked at not as groups or generations, but as individuals with their own interests, likes, dislikes, and personal needs. Relationships must be built with each individual, and love must be shown.

Recommendations for Greater Impact

This project will only make a limited difference if it remains primarily the study of one church's introduction of a program of outreach-oriented small groups. Therefore, I would like to suggest recommendations for the following groups of people who have the potential to greatly impact the areas examined in this project:

1. To the academic community responsible for undergraduate education of pastors, I recommend that you allow for practical training in small group leadership. It is not enough to share the academic importance of group life if there is no room for putting it into practice. The small group I led in college for other collegiate students was foundational in my small group understanding.

2. To the administrative organizations of the Seventh-day Adventist Church, I recommend that you continually cast a vision for evangelism. It is easy for pastors and churches to get caught in the busyness of a church calendar. Challenge the pastors to strive for involving all members, young and old, in sharing the gospel. Outreach-oriented small groups are one way that can happen.

3. To the Seventh-day Adventist Theological Seminary, I recommend that you continue to offer fields of study that specifically address the growth of the church. I greatly appreciated this "Evangelism and Church Growth Cohort" and the ability to direct this study in a course for the expansion of God's kingdom. Please make sure that assignments are truly meaningful for the professional and personal growth of those being trained.

4. To young pastors with a passion for youth and evangelism, I recommend that you continue to pass this passion along to young people. I urge you to move beyond the ministry of entertaining young people, and develop even better tools to equip youth for the work on ministry. Remember that young people can be more than targets of evangelism, but can be powerful partners in outreach.

5. To young people who are searching for your place in the church, I recommend that you don't give up! God has a place for you to impact the world, starting with the people around you. Look for others with whom you can pray, study the Bible, share your faith, and grow together in your Christian life. Then find the place that you can best reach the world.

Ongoing Impact of GROWgroups

Even though this project is complete, GROWgroups are still taking place at GCA Church. In the current semester, along with several groups led by church members, at least four groups totally led by students have recently begun, and are practically full. It seems that the vision for groups is finding a place in the church and the momentum for groups is continuing to grow. This momentum seems to be growing as young people are not only participating in groups, but taking an active role leadership in the groups, as well as recruiting fellow students to encourage participation. Students are leading other students into community with each other and with Jesus, and outreach events continue to take place.

These groups continue to play a key role in the mission of the GCA Church. This church adapted a 3-fold Discipleship Plan to lead students to *Know*, *Grow*, and *Go*. GROWgroups helped to fulfill this Discipleship plan. Groups are a significant aspect of an individual knowing God better through the Bible and fellowship. Through the GROWgroup process, both leaders and group members are being trained and are growing in their gifts and talents as they find places to serve in the church. And finally, through the GROWgroup emphasis on service and outreach, these groups aim to help engage participants in evangelistic outreach and service to go into the community and the world.

Personal Growth

The intense process of completing this ministry project was a vast learning experience. Many things learned have already been mentioned. But one does not undertake a project like this without absorbing things in a more personal matter. This process has made changes in my life and ministry that will continue on long after this project is completed.

One area of personal growth was in discovering a renewed belief in the importance of small groups in the life and ministry of the church. During seminary studies earlier in life, I caught a vision for small groups, but in my previous role as chaplain, it was difficult to cast that vision into the life of the church. But through the implementation of this project, and with a new pastoral position, I was able to begin the process of instilling a small group mentality into a church that did not previously have small groups as a part of their church.

The process of sharing the vision with church leaders, casting the vision to church members and students, and recruiting and training group leaders, has helped me to once again see the importance of people growing in community together. I see members and students excited about groups, taking on new challenges of leadership, and learning and growing their talents and skills for God.

A second area of personal growth that this project helped me with is in gaining perseverance. It is easy in ministry to set small goals that are quickly accomplished and then set aside for the next thing. But through this process of adding a significant area of ministry into the life of a church, I have seen that this is a long process. It does not come quickly or easily. Mistakes are made and lessons learned. But through it all, the project continues with a specific goal in mind. That goal helps with evaluation, reconfiguration, and inspiration throughout the months and years of working toward success.

A final area of ministry that this project helped to surface is a passion for equipping people for ministry. This is a primary role of the pastor (Eph 4:11, 12), and yet one that is often neglected. But if a program for small groups is to be successful in a local congregation, it takes more than one pastor or leader. Group leaders must be trained, equipped, and given authority and permission to lead their group in a way that works best for them. They probably will not always do it the same way that I would, and I am fine with that because it means that someone else is engaged in ministry and is using their spiritual gifts.

I have learned anew that equipping is also an ongoing process. Equipping is more than just sharing knowledge, but it also must have a practical application. Follow up is needed, questions need to be answered, and encouragement must be given. But the time investment is well worth it because it is fulfilling the mission of "equipping the saints for the work of ministry." As a result of this renewed determination to equip, I have recently started *EquipPodcast* (Hudson, 2016), an audio podcast for the purpose of inspiring church members and leaders to find ways to get every member involved in ministry and strive for Total Member Involvement (McKey, 2016). This podcast will be an ongoing and growing resource after this project is completed.

Conclusion

The goal of this project was the development of a church-wide system of small groups for students and church members of the GCA Church. The purpose of these GROWgroups was to meet the relational needs of members of the Millennial generation while challenging them to look beyond themselves and to be engaged in witnessing to the community. A church that did not have small groups now has an ongoing focus on groups meeting together. Young people saw and experienced small groups based on biblical principles of community. They were trained to use their gifts, both in group leadership and neighborhood outreach. Various forms of outreach activities were developed to meet the needs in the neighborhoods around the school and to give students an opportunity to serve beyond the walls of the church, both in transformational and proclamational outreach.

Small groups provided a place of community for students to be trained, equipped, and inspired for service. This project describes a process for developing small groups on an academy campus church that could be utilized by other Adventist churches and schools for both members and students.

There is more that can be learned regarding small groups and outreach, but this project sets forth a foundation for others to build upon. It is hoped that others will find this research and development process to be helpful in the formation of small groups in other contexts for the purpose of equipping young people to help fulfill the Great Commission. As students know more about God and grow in their gifts and talents, they are ready and able to go and make a difference in the world.

APPENDIX A

SMALL GROUP STRATEGY INTERVIEWS

Phone Interview with Pastor Dan Serns
Richardson, Texas Seventh-day Adventist Church
December 4, 2015 – 1 hour interview

What is Your Church membership/attendance?

Pastor of Richardson, Texas, Seventh-day Adventist Church.
Membership – 940. Attendance – 650-700. Sanctuary seats only 375
2 Services and overflow in Sabbath School rooms. Have planted multiple churches in last few years

Do you have an intentional small group strategy and what does it look like:
Yes, everyone is better off in a group or a number of groups.

Lots of types of groups – Sabbath School, Ministry, Bible study, Mission

Each group has 1 key leader, but needs 3 leaders – Up reach, In reach, Outreach, as well as board mentor. Church board mentors are listed in bulletin each week. All board members are to mentor either groups or people. Mentor to listen to ideas, give council and advice … not to do the work. They represent the group on the board.

If God has put a burden on your heart, YOU do something.

Each Group needs – 1) Connect with God, 2) Find partner or two to start ministry, 3) Find a coach (board mentor), 4) Flock – people in your group to serve

Partners is what makes group sustainable: 1) Main leader (upreach) to direct toward God. 2) Inreach – Connect group to each other. 3) Outreach – who are we working for to bring to Jesus

Challenge each group to bring people to Jesus and Advent movement

We use "Groups" in large sense of word – 3-12 people, but many types – Choir, Pathfinders, Sabbath School (if too big, broken up into smaller groups)

Like *Activate* – Start all on same week, 3 cycles per year

At end of each groups session there is a week long reaping series, our Harvest Cycle ... often lead by one of the groups

A Key - Every 4th Sabbath – Fill the baptistery Sabbath. Look at groups and see who is ready for baptism. In 71 months, had at least 1 baptsm 63 months. Helps keep focus ... if no baptism, why not? What do we need to do different?

Some things different than most - Groups run on Trimester, but can start anytime they have leaders and mentor.

Allow anyone to be a group leader (even non-Adventist) – with leaders and mentor.

Wide-open – sometimes people disappointed when no one shows up. Group leaders need to recruit their group, even if just a small number.

Board mentors – all board members mentor either people or a group.

Mentors need mentors – during church board meetings, go into huddles – Elders mentor the mentors during 15 minutes of church board meeting.

Groups can meet anywhere – any place, any time. Some examples
Sunday AM – Rec Center – Devotional and Bible Study
Wednesday after school for young people – baptismal class (Amazing Adventures)
Start 1 new Sabbath School group each year – EGW – Sabbath School is greatest missionary organization in church

How many groups do you have? How many people involved, what percentage of your congregation?
Our goal is that group number equals 10% of attendance (i.e., 650 attending = 65 groups)

We have about 65 – 75 groups.

Homes of Hope - provide lessons and yard sign for people to meet in neighborhood for 1 quarter – Health/Great Hope

Percentage of church that participate – unsure exactly. Total of 600-700 (but some are in multiple groups)

Who else would you recommend I talk to about small group strategy?
Spanish churches – different concept of groups – small groups designed to move to evangelistic meetings. Ask Roger Hernandez (Southern Union Evangelism Coordinator and mutual friend) for suggestions of which churches to ask.

Tyler Bower – Fort Worth First (Uses *Activate* style groups)

Phone Interview with Pastor Rodlie Ortiz
Pioneer Memorial Church, Associate Pastor for Outreach/Evangelism
December 10, 2015 – 45 min interview

What is your church membership/Attendance?
We have membership of about 3,800. Our attendance is around 1,800.

Do you have an intentional small group strategy, and if you do, what is it?
Yes, we are very intentional with small groups. We feel they are a core piece of discipleship delivery. Our full discipleship process is Connect, Serve, Grow, Go, and GROWgroups (our term for small groups) is a major part of the Grow segment.

We have been involved with GROWgroups for about 3 years, and it remains a central piece of our plan. We follow the model from the book *Activate* (by Nelson Searcy) very closely. Therefore our groups are Affinity groups that range from Disc Golf to Daniel.

We promote small groups following the Activate model, using Form, Fill, etc.
We have 3 weeks of promotion (right after the beginning of the school year). We place a catalog of groups in every bulletin for a few weeks. Pastor Dwight Nelson references the groups in at least one of his sermons.

A big part of our promotion process is using connect cards. We use them every week. We use them to find leader volunteers. Then during our promotion weeks, people can sign up for GROWgroups right on the Connect Card. They can also use our website.

Leadership is a key. This was first launched with Esther Knott was pastor of Discipleship (and she was here for 1½ years). Then we had interim and GROWgroup responsibility added to other pastors workload. You could notice a downturn. Our new pastor of Discipleship is Sabine Vatel. Process is growing again with good leadership.

All the pastors lead out in a group, including Pastor Dwight.

Leader Training/Orientation. Very simple. We have dinner with GROWgroup leaders shortly before the kick-off. Group leaders are introduced to Team Leader (team leader oversees several group leaders). Group leaders are to bring a brief syllabus of what will be covered/what the group will do each week, including when is the outreach/social event. Then the pastor will share a few group leading pointers.

Team leaders each lead 5 group leaders. They contact every week, and host them for a meal twice each semester just to check in. The pastor oversees the Team Leaders.

We follow *Activate* very closely.

How many groups do you have? How many people in groups?
We have about 50 groups with about 600 people.

What impact on outreach does your small group strategy have?
Outreach is a key element of the GROWgroup process. Each group is expected to have at least one meeting for outreach (and one social event). Pastor Sabine oversees, but groups make their own decisions about what outreach they do. The church provides some suggestions or ideas, but each group does its own thing.

My group has worked at the Pregnancy Care Center, we have adopted a family. With 50 or so groups doing differing things, it really does make an impact on the community.

Is there anything I did not ask you that is important to understanding small groups in your church?
Our church uses software called "Church Teams," which helps to connect leaders. Each group leader has a team leader. Team leaders supervise 5 group leaders. Every week the group leader gets automated e-mail from the team leader. It asks some simple questions: Did you meet this week? Describe your group experience. This is a simple two minute process. If e-mail is ignored, another is sent. If ignored three times, discipleship pastor is contacted and able to step in and see what the problem is. This is great for accountability

Some groups don't get filled. It is crowd-sourced, groups fill up and people have an interest. If not filled, sometimes those leaders get their feelings hurt, but soon realize that it is not about them.

Summer is a slow semester in our academic setting. Students are gone, professors and pastors often take vacation. We still have groups during the summer, but don't emphasize as much. We usually have about 20 groups in the summer.

One of the biggest blessings is that people get to know new people. In a big church you may not know someone or may have never even seen them. This gives the opportunity to meet a few new people every semester.

Do you know another church that has successful groups that you would suggest I talk to?
David Asscherick is using a similar strategy in his church in Australia.

Tom Evans at NADEI is trying to connect with all churches in NAD that are following this model.

APPENDIX B

QUESTIONNAIRES

GROWgroup Project Pre-Survey
(Surveys are anonymous. Do NOT put name or any identification on this survey.)

1. **Age**   0-16   17-24   25-39   40-65   65+

2. **Rate the following aspects of your personal experience:**

   Personal Spirituality:
   Not Important   1   2   3   4   5   Very Important

   Outreach Experience:
   No Experience   1   2   3   4   5   Very Experienced

   Outreach Skills:
   No Skills   1   2   3   4   5   Very Skilled

3. ***I pray:***
   1 - Never
   2 - Once or twice a week
   3 - Once a day
   4 - Several Times a Day

4. ***I read or study the Bible:***
   1 - Never
   2 - Ten hours or less a <u>year</u>
   3 - About 1 to 2 hours a <u>month</u>
   4 - About 1 hour a <u>week</u>
   5 - About 15 to 30 minutes a <u>day</u>
   6 - More than 30 minutes a <u>day</u>

   For questions 5 through 11, please use the following scale:
   1 – Never
   2 – Very Rarely
   3 – Rarely
   4 - Often
   5 - Frequently
   6 – Very Frequently

5. ***I work with other Christian believers for the purpose of introducing unchurched people to Jesus Christ:***
   (Never)   1   2   3   4   5   6   (Very Frequently)

6. ***Based on my abilities and spiritual gifts, I assist in some way in the teaching ministry of my church.***
   (Never)   1   2   3   4   5   6   (Very Frequently)

7. *I invite unchurched people to attend church or small-group meetings with me.
   (Never)   1   2   3   4   5   6   (Very Frequently)

8. *I pray for people and/or organizations that are working for the salvation of the unsaved.
   (Never)   1   2   3   4   5   6   (Very Frequently)

9. *When someone is my church is sick or experiences some other problem and needs me, I help them.
   (Never)   1   2   3   4   5   6   (Very Frequently)

10. *I meet with a small group of Christian friends for prayer, Bible study, or ministry.
    (Never)   1   2   3   4   5   6   (Very Frequently)

11. *I serve in a church ministry or community agency to help people in need.
    (Never)   1   2   3   4   5   6   (Very Frequently)

12. How would you rate your current spiritual health? (1 = nonexistent, 10 = thriving)

13. Why have you chosen to participate in GROWgroups?

14. What aspects of GROWgroups excite you?

15. What aspects of GROWgroups concern you?

---

* These questions adapted from Thayer, J. (1999). *The Christian Spiritual Participation Profile*. Jane Thayer.

GROWgroup Project Post-Survey
(Surveys are anonymous. Do NOT put name or any identification on this survey.)

1. **Age**   0-16   17-24   25-39   40-65   65+

2. **Rate the following aspects of your personal experience:**

    Personal Spirituality:
    Not Important   1   2   3   4   5   Very Important

    Outreach Experience:
    No Experience   1   2   3   4   5   Very Experienced

    Outreach Skills:
    No Skills   1   2   3   4   5   Very Skilled

3. ***I pray:**
    1 - Never
    2 - Once or twice a week
    3 - Once a day
    4 - Several Times a Day

4. ***I read or study the Bible:**
    1 - Never
    2 - Ten hours or less a <u>year</u>
    3 - About 1 to 2 hours a <u>month</u>
    4 - About 1 hour a <u>week</u>
    5 - About 15 to 30 minutes a <u>day</u>
    6 - More than 30 minutes a <u>day</u>

For questions 5 through 11, please use the following scale:
   1 – Never   4 - Often
   2 – Very Rarely   5 - Frequently
   3 – Rarely   6 – Very Frequently

5. ***I work with other Christian believers for the purpose of introducing unchurched people to Jesus Christ:**
   (Never)   1   2   3   4   5   6   (Very Frequently)

6. ***Based on my abilities and spiritual gifts, I assist in some way in the teaching ministry of my church.**
   (Never)   1   2   3   4   5   6   (Very Frequently)

7. ***I invite unchurched people to attend church or small-group meetings with me.**
   (Never)   1   2   3   4   5   6   (Very Frequently)

8. ***I pray for people and/or organizations that are working for the salvation of the unsaved.**
   (Never)   1   2   3   4   5   6   (Very Frequently)

9. *When someone is my church is sick or experiences some other problem and needs me, I help them.
    (Never)   1   2   3   4   5   6   (Very Frequently)

10. *I meet with a small group of Christian friends for prayer, Bible study, or ministry.
    (Never)   1   2   3   4   5   6   (Very Frequently)

11. *I serve in a church ministry or community agency to help people in need.
    (Never)   1   2   3   4   5   6   (Very Frequently)

12. I participated in a GROWgroup this school year:
    1 - Yes   2 - No

13. Do you feel the GROWgroup program provided adequate opportunity for evangelism training?
    1 - Yes   2 - No

14. Do you feel the GROWgroup program provided adequate opportunity for Active Outreach?
    1 - Yes   2 - No

15. Do you feel the GROWgroup program provided adequate opportunity for small group interaction?
    1 - Yes   2 - No

16. On a scale of 1-10, rate the following areas pertaining to how you feel GROWgroup has benefited you (1= negative experience; 5= Not at all benefited; 10 = greatly benefited)

    Emotionally

    Spiritually

    Evangelistically

    Socially

17. How would you rate your current spiritual health? (1 = nonexistent, 10 = thriving)

---

* These questions adapted from Thayer, J. (1999). *The Christian Spiritual Participation Profile.* Jane Thayer.

APPENDIX C

COMMUNITY LEADER INTERVIEWS

Interview Questions for Community Leaders (Sahlin, 2004):

1. What are the biggest assets and strong points of your community? What services does your organization provide?
2. My church wants to help with some of the most important needs in your community. What are some of the important needs you think might be good for us to focus on?
3. What could a church group do that would be helpful in the needs you have mentioned? (Go through the list item by item and ask for specific suggestions for each one.)
4. Who are some of the influential leaders in the community we should interview with the same questions? Do you have contact information for them? May I tell them you referred me?

Community Leader Interview Outlines

Denise Rustad
Director of Creation Health, Gordon Hospital
Interview on December 17, 2015

What are the biggest assets and strong points of your community? What services does your organization provide?

One of the assets is to have a quality hospital in a small community. Also we have companies, businesses, and manufacturers who are really interested in the health of their employees. They want to provide was for people to be healthy.

We provide education. We have classes twice a year. These are eight week sessions to provide teaching on the CREATION health principles

We have a Farmers' Market every week during the summer and fall. This helps the community growers, and gives a place for people to buy fresh produce. During the Farmers' Market we provide recipes to help people use their health produce to make actual meals.

We also do events at the local schools for health education.

What are some of the important needs you think might be good for us to focus on?
Finances are a big need. People can't afford their health care, some even can't afford the gas to come to hospital for chemo and other needs.

There is also the lack of desire. It doesn't matter about having keys to health if people aren't interested. We look for ways to peak interest, so people will desire life change. Many aren't interested until it is too late.

What could a church group do that would be helpful in the needs you have mentioned?
I think the use of young people could help a lot. Community members love to see young people involved in positive things, even raking leaves. They may not listen to them give scientific reasons for health choices, but by example and attitude. Young people could do fun things with younger ones, games and activities. They could act as mentors in this way.

Who are some of the influential leaders in the community we should interview with the same questions?
Tracy Farriba

Mary Mayes, Director
Imagination Station, Calhoun, Georgia
Interview on December 16, 2015

What are the biggest assets and strong points of your community? What services does your organization provide?
The school system does a good job. The children have the opportunity to get a quality education.

We are a place for kids to come after school. Right now we have over 40. They come as a place to be, a place to do home work, to socialize, to stay out of trouble. They are able to be here for several hours.

What are some of the important needs you think might be good for us to focus on?
There are challenges with tutoring. These kids have a hard time with times tables. Also with having people set positive examples in their lives – mentoring. Getting enough exercise is an ongoing challenge. Funding is always a challenge for an organization like ours, although we do have donors that are willing to help.

What could a church group do that would be helpful in the needs you have mentioned?
Well, if we had people, students, or adults that could help with tutoring. Even something as simple as times tables. We would love to have someone come and teach these students how to Double Dutch. They can't even jump a single rope very many

times. It is good for exercise. We need different ways to exercise. We are looking to put in a volleyball court. Some of your students helped with cleaning before. We are hoping that can continue. Any help we can get!

Vickie Spence, Director
United Way of Calhoun/Gordon County

What are the biggest assets and strong points of your community? What services does your organization provide?

The people! They are willing to help if they see a real need. The city and county really work to help the organizations meet needs and are willing to step out and make a difference. There is not a lot of territorialism among the organizations (most of the time). Also the faith community work to meet needs. Sometimes working with the pastors isn't the best, but you can find Sunday Schools that are willing to help.

We connect those in need with those that can help. We help the organizations raise funds. This year there are 18 organizations that work with us. We raise money to help the organizations function, then help tie everything together.

What are some of the important needs you think might be good for us to focus on?

There are so many that we see. Mental health is a big need in this area. There just isn't much help for that. Also transportation is needed. Not just for the elderly, so many people are on bikes and have a hard time getting where they need to be. There is a lack of women's health providers, especially affordable. Drugs is an ongoing issue in our community. Also homelessness is much more prevalent than you would think for a small community.

What could a church group do that would be helpful in the needs you have mentioned?

They could certainly help with finances. If we had a group we could turn to when there is a small need to be met, that could help. Your church is very well educated. Your doctors could meet a huge need in this area. Working at the free clinic. But also there could be health education that is needed, with both your members and students.

Who are some of the influential leaders in the community we should interview with the same questions?
Roberta Charbaneax

Nancy Soto, Executive Director
Voluntary Action Center, Calhoun, GA

What are the biggest assets and strong points of your community? What services does your organization provide?

People of this community do pull together to meet needs. Government, individuals, and Faith Communities all help to sponsor this organization.

The Voluntary Action Center (VAC) does many things. We have daily lunch, during weekdays, that anyone can eat at, no screening required. We also provide washer and dryer, and shower facilities with no screening needed. We have a screening process and help people with utilities, rent, etc. We also have a food and clothes bank to meet needs. We have a thrift store that anyone can shop at to help fund some of these projects. We have The Bridge program that helps people find a place to stay (currently in motels because our county has no homeless shelter).

What are some of the important needs you think might be good for us to focus on?
Some of the biggest needs we have in this community involves transportation. People can't get or keep a job if they don't have reliable way to get to work. There is also a huge need with child care. Most of the day cares in this community don't go past 5 or 6 pm. If someone has a shift that goes until 7, they don't have a place for there kids. They can't break the cycle of poor choices if they aren't able to get that start. Our organization has huge financial needs. We get grants, but that doesn't cover our working expenses to pay the case-workers and others who can help with our needs.

What could a church group do that would be helpful in the needs you have mentioned?
Financial help would be great. As mentioned before that is one of our biggest needs. Volunteers are also needed. To help with daily lunches. We have facilities if some would like to do training/education on basic budgeting and finances, health education, creating a resume', and things like that.

Who are some of the influential leaders in the community we should interview with the same questions?
Vickie Spence or Roberta Charbaneaux

APPENDIX D

Reach the World LESSONS

Reach the World LESSON 1
Outside/Inside

Life in Action:
Hudson Taylor. Born in 1832, Hudson early left the Christian faith of his parents. But at the age of 17, Hudson gave his heart to Christ and soon committed his life to going as a missionary to China. He studied medicine and lived among the poor, working to win people to Jesus. He finally arrived in China in 1854 at the age of 22. Hudson spent most of the next 51 years ministering in China over the course of 11 different missionary tours.

He survived civil wars, riots, and the untimely death of several loved ones. Known as a man of prayer and of the Bible, Taylor founded the China Inland Mission, which sent hundreds of missionaries to China and became the largest Protestant missionary organization.

"Hudson Taylor was, ...one of the greatest missionaries of all time, and ... one of the four or five most influential foreigners who came to China in the nineteenth century for any purpose..." -Kenneth Scott Latourette (https://en.wikipedia.org/wiki/Hudson_Taylor)

Reach the World
Basic Training #1

The Commission

"For God so loved the world that he gave his only begotten Son ..."

Jesus lived and died on this earth, so that all people will have the opportunity to accept his grace and salvation. He came to "seek and to save the lost." As we eagerly wait for the 2nd Coming of Jesus, what is the role of the church and the individual Christian in sharing the message of Jesus with our community, family, and friends.

This series will explore that concept and discover practical ways to share in God's mission on earth.

GROUP ACTION:
In what area can we make a difference for Jesus this school year? (A particular neighborhood, a city, a park, etc.)

What would it mean to accomplish this mission in this context?

What might it look look like to GO? To MAKE DISCIPLE? To BAPTIZE? To TEACH?

(The group will begin to formulate a plan of action over the next several weeks)

MY ACTION:
If I don't know, I will ask someone in my family the story about how we became an Adventist Christian

Pray for ....

_____
_____
_____
_____

What is a disciple? Disciple - (noun) -
1. **Any professed follower of Christ in His lifetime.**
2. **Any follower of Christ** (dictionary.com)

Launch

-Share the story of a "great" project you completed. Was it a success or a failure? Why?

-Tell the story of the first person in you family to become an Adventist (or a Christian)? (Was it you, a parent, your grandparents?)

Call to Action
Matthew 28:16-20

"Then the eleven disciples went away into Galilee, to the mountain which Jesus had appointed for them. "When they saw Him, they worshiped Him; but some doubted.

"And Jesus came and spoke to them, saying, "All authority has been given to Me in heaven and on earth. "Go therefore and make disciples of all the nations, baptizing them in the name of the Father and of the Son and of the Holy Spirit, "teaching them to observe all things that I have commanded you; and lo, I am with you always, even to the end of the age." Amen.

"It is the privilege of every Christian not only to look for but to hasten the coming our Lord Jesus Christ." - *Christ's Object Lessons*, 69.

Reflection

-What is the context of this story?

-Who is here?

-"They worshipped, but some doubted" (17). Why do you think some disciples still doubted? Why did Jesus still give this Great Commission to them?

-What is the first statement that Jesus makes (18)?

-What do you think it means that Jesus has "all authority"?

-Jesus give 4 commands: Go, make disciples, baptize, teach. Which of those do you find most exciting? Most challenging? Most important? Why?

(Note that the main verb in the sentence is GO ... The other three relate back to "going")

-Jesus instructs His disciples to make disciples. What does that mean for us, as disciples today?

-"Surely I am with always"- what reaction do you think the disciples had to this statement? What reaction do you have?

Reach the World LESSON 2
Outside/Inside

Reach the World
Basic Training #2
Power to Witness

Life in Action:
In 1970, a small group of students at Asbury College in Kentucky had been praying for revival on that campus. Unexpectedly, at a routine chapel service, a spirit of confession and repentance swept over the gathered student body. Students shared testimony, confessed sins, and wept together. Meals were skipped, classes suspended as the campus shared and prayed together. Classes were canceled for the rest of the week at Bible study and prayer groups met across campus. This revival soon spread to other college campus. In just a few months, a similar revival sprung up on the campus of Andrews University, as students gave their hearts to Jesus, and the campus was a blaze with revival fires. And these fires spread to other campuses, Oakwood College, Atlantic Union, Mt. Vernon Academy. Changing the hearts and lives of students and teachers, so they could change the lives of family and friends, so they could change the lives of people in their community. All because some young people were praying for a revival. Could it happen again?
~from Dwight Nelson
https://www.pmchurch.org/blog/2010/09/15/what-if-god-repeated-himself-every-forty-years

GROUP ACTION:
Begin to pray for three things:
1) Pray for the members of this group, that as individuals they will be filled with Holy Spirit and ready to serve God.

2) Pray for revival at your church/school. May many others desire to serve God and the community.

3) Pray for ministry opportunities for this group to participate in

MY ACTION:
Make a list of people that you associate with:
A. Family
B. Close Friends
C. Work/School Associates
D. Causal Acquaintances

- What can you do to begin to influence each group for Jesus?

"Then those who gladly received his word were baptized, and that day about three thousand souls were added to them." Acts 2:41

As Jesus ascended to heaven at the close of His earthly ministry, he left the disciples with a mission, and Jesus left them with the Gift of the Holy Spirit. Soon they were reaching the world. The early church used this power and took the message of the Love of God to the world. This study will look at how the early church responded the promise of the Spirit, and will examine if it it possible for us to do the same thing today?

"Since this is the means by which we are to receive power, why do we not hunger and thirst for the gift of the Spirit? Why do we not talk of it, pray for it, and preach concerning it? .... For the daily baptism of the Spirit every worker should offer his petition to God. Companies of Christian workers should gather to ask for special help, for heavenly wisdom, that they may know how to plan and execute wisely." -*Acts of the Apostles*, 50.

Launch

- Describe one of your good friends from 1st grade. What do you remember about them?

-What topic has been "trending" in your life in the last week (school, sports, music, etc.)? What have you been talking about the most?

Call to Action
Acts 1:4-8

⁴ And being assembled together with *them*, He commanded them not to depart from Jerusalem, but to wait for the Promise of the Father, "which," *He* said, "you have heard from Me; ⁵ for John truly baptized with water, but you shall be baptized with the Holy Spirit not many days from now." ⁶ Therefore, when they had come together, they asked Him, saying, "Lord, will You at this time restore the kingdom to Israel?" ⁷ And He said to them, "It is not for you to know times or seasons which the Father has put in His own authority. ⁸ But you shall receive power when the Holy Spirit has come upon you; and you shall be witnesses to Me in Jerusalem, and in all Judea and Samaria, and to the end of the earth."

Morning by morning, as the heralds of the gospel kneel before the Lord and renew their vows of consecration to Him, He will grant them the presence of His Spirit, with its reviving, sanctifying power.
- *Acts of the Apostles*, 56.

Reflection

- When in the timeline of Jesus' life did this story take place?

- How do you think the disciples felt when Jesus said, "It is not for you to know the times or seasons" (7)?

-Jesus said the disciples would receive power from the Holy Spirit to be witnesses. Think of some examples from the Bible when this power was exhibited (Pentecost, etc.).

What did the disciples do as they waited for the Holy Spirit? (see Acts 1:14)

-What do you think it means to receive power from the Holy Spirit?

-Does this promise of Holy Spirit power relate to us today? (see John 14:12)

-Notice the locations that are mentioned (8): This verse is a condensed version of the rest of the book of Acts:
  a. Jerusalem - Acts 1-7
  b. Judea - Acts 8:1-3
  c. Samaria - Acts 8-10
  d. The ends of the earth
        - Acts 11- 28

-What "circles of influence" in your life correlate with the expanding targets of ministry mentioned.

-What would it look like for this group to pray like the disciples?

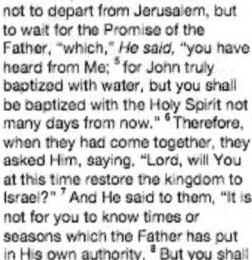

Reach the World LESSON 3
Outside/Inside

Life in Action:
Battle Creek, 1868.
A request had come for missionaries to visit the American West, especially California. At the General Conference, an appeal was made, "Has no one any impression of the duty to the California field?"

Daniel T. Bourdeau (1835 - 1905) rose from his seat. He was willing to go. He was ready to go. Together with his wife, they had sold their home and most of their belongings. They had arrived at Battle Creek with all they owned in a wooden chest, prepared to go wherever the Lord would send them. They soon set sail for California along with another missionary couple. Together they planted the first Adventist churches west of the Rocky Mountains

(Collins, Norma, Heart-warming Stories of the Pioneers, 174).

Reach the World
Basic Training #3

The Harvest is Great

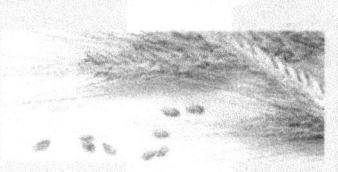

There are over 7 billion people in the world. Over 2 billion of them have probably never even heard of Jesus. There are over 350 million people in the US. The growth rate of the Adventist church is barely keeping up with the growth rate of the country. Anyway you look at it, every where you look, there are LOTS of people that need to hear the good news of Salvation in Jesus. Who is going to tell them?

Paul writes, "Preach the word! Be ready in season and out of season. Convince, rebuke, exhort, with all longsuffering and teaching" (2 Tim 4:2). All of us are called to share with someone else. There are many people that need to hear about Jesus. There are many ways to share your faith.

Are you ready to help?

GROUP ACTION:

-Pray daily for each member of this group, that they will be "laborers sent into the harvest."

-Spend Time praying for God to grant you "holy boldness" (See Acts 4:13, 31, that you may be willing to make a difference for God.

MY ACTION:

-Take a Spiritual Gifts Test and Pray that God will show where to best use your spiritual gifts

-Pray that your eyes will be open to see people that are interested in learning more about spiritual truths.

"Representations passed before me of a **great reformatory movement among God's people**.... The **spirit of intercession** was seen.... **Hundreds were seen** visiting families and opening before them the word of God. Hearts were convicted by the **power of the Holy Spirit**, and a spirit of genuine conversion was manifest. On every side doors were thrown open to the proclamation of the truth." *Testimonies for the Church*, Vol, 9, 126.

Launch

-Have you ever planted a garden or had a houseplant? Describe how it turned out.

- What was best "team" you were ever on (sports, work, school, etc.)? What did you accomplish, what made it successful?

Call to Action
Matt 9:35-38

35 Then Jesus went about all the cities and villages, teaching in their synagogues, preaching the gospel of the kingdom, and healing every sickness and every disease among the people. 36 But when He saw the multitudes, He was moved with compassion for them, because they were weary and scattered, like sheep having no shepherd. 37 Then He said to His disciples, "The harvest truly *is* plentiful, but the laborers *are* few. 38 Therefore pray the Lord of the harvest to send out laborers into His harvest."

John 4:34, 35
34 Jesus said to them, "My food is to do the will of Him who sent Me, and to finish His work. 35 Do you not say, 'There are still four months and *then* comes the harvest'? Behold, I say to you, lift up your eyes and look at the fields, for they are already white for harvest!

"Strength to resist evil is best gained through aggressive service"
~ *Acts of the Apostles*, 105.

Reflection

-What evidence do you see in the world today that "the harvest is great"?

-Jesus said in John 4:35, "The fields are already white for the harvest." Do you think that is more or less true today than in the days of Jesus? Why?

-What do think Jesus meant with his request to pray for laborers to be sent out?

-Do you think of yourself as a laborer? Why or why not?

-Read the following verses:
Isaiah 6:8 - *Also I heard the voice of the Lord, saying: "Whom shall I send, And who will go for Us?" Then I said, "Here am I! Send me."*

Matthew 5:13 - 16 - *You are the salt of the earth ... You are the light of the world ... Let your light so shine before men, that they may see your good works and glorify your Father in heaven.*

-How do these verses challenge all Christians to be "labors" for God?

Reach the World LESSON 4
Outside/Inside

Stories in Action:

Women at the Well - *"Come, see a Man who told me all things that I ever did. Could this be the Christ?" Then they went out of the city and came to Him.*
— John 4

Peter - *"You are a chosen generation, a royal priesthood, a holy nation, His own special people, that you may proclaim the praises of Him who called you out of darkness into His marvelous light."*
— 1 Peter 2

Paul - *O wretched man that I am! Who will deliver me from this body of death? I thank God—through Jesus Christ our Lord! .... There is therefore now no condemnation to those who are in Christ Jesus*
— Romans 7 & 8

John - *That which we have seen and heard we declare to you, that you also may have fellowship with us; and truly our fellowship is with the Father and with His Son Jesus Christ.*
— 1 John 1

Reach the World
Basic Training #4

What to Say

"And they overcame him by the blood of the Lamb, and the word of their testimony." Revelation 12:11

What do you do when your team wins the big game? When that special someone asks you out? When you get a perfect score on the big test? When you make the big sale at work? Usually, when something amazing happens in your life, you tell someone about it! "Did you see that catch!?!?" ... "You won't believe what happened!!

We want to share good news. That is your story, your testimony. Sharing your story about how God had impacted your life can make a big difference in someone else's life!

GROUP ACTION:
As seen in this study, God can use anyone. God can use you!

1) Practice sharing your testimony with others in the group (see "My Action").

2) Take a Spiritual Gift Test to see areas of potential ministry skills in your life

3) Determine how your skills and talents can be used, and start to put them in action!

MY ACTION:
How Can I share my story? Complete 3 statements:

-My Life before I met Jesus was ... (What were some spiritual challenges?)

-I met Jesus ... (when/why did Jesus become a relevant part of your life?)

-Now my life is ... (How is your life different now? What part does Jesus play in your life now? Peace, hope, etc.)

Witness - Both the one sharing a testimony and the proclamation itself come from the same Greek root. We know the word as "martyr" ... Someone who proclaims their message by the way they live (and sometimes die). You ARE a "witness" ... What story are you sharing?

Launch

- Describe an interesting place you have visited.

- Share how you have seen God at work (in your life, school, family, etc.) over the last week.

Call to Action
Luke 8:35-39

³⁵ Then they went out to see what had happened, and came to Jesus, and found the man from whom the demons had departed, sitting at the feet of Jesus, clothed and in his right mind. And they were afraid. ³⁶ They also who had seen it told them by what means he who had been demon-possessed was healed. ³⁷ Then the whole multitude of the surrounding region of the Gadarenes asked Him to depart from them, for they were seized with great fear. And He got into the boat and returned. ³⁸ Now the man from whom the demons had departed begged Him that he might be with Him. But Jesus sent him away, saying, ³⁹ "Return to your own house, and tell what great things God has done for you." And he went his way and proclaimed throughout the whole city what great things Jesus had done for him.

Reflection

-What was the spiritual condition of the man on the seashore? (:27)

-What was his condition when the people returned from town? (:35)

-How long do you imagine the healed man was with Jesus that day?

-What did the man ask of Jesus? (:38)

-This is one of the only people that Jesus didn't allow to stay with him. Jesus apparently saw that the man could do a great work for God.

-What did Jesus tell the man to do? (:39)

-How do you think the man felt when Jesus gave him this mission?

-The next time Jesus came to this region, the people flocked to him and wanted to learn more. (See Matthew 15:30)

-Apparently this man made a big impact. In the morning he had been possessed by a demon. He spent one day with Jesus. And he had a story to tell.

-What story do you have to tell?

It is in working to spread the good news of salvation that we are brought near to the Saviour .... If we have been following Jesus step by step, we shall have something right to the point to tell.
— The Desire of Ages, 340.

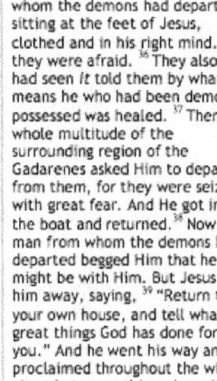

Reach the World LESSON 5
Outside/Inside

Life in Action:
Anna Knight, Teacher/Missionary

Anna Knight (1874-1972) was born in Mississippi. As a young girl, she received Adventist reading material and was soon baptized. She attended Mt. Vernon Academy, and then the School of Nursing at Battle Creek College.

Anna lived her life to help others. She opened a school in Mississippi for underprivileged children. After a few years, she received a call to go to India as the first Black woman missionary of any denomination. In India for five years, Anna was involved in education, evangelism, health ministry, and agriculture education. From there she returned to the US and worked in Mississippi, Georgia, Oakwood, and across the South in education and outreach work. She lived to be 98 years old, dedicating her life to meeting the needs of others.

Source: http://www.oakwood.edu/historyportal/Research/StudentBio/knightX25A.htm

Reach the World
Basic Training #5
Christ's Method Alone

COMPASSION
compassionmovement.org

GROUP ACTION:
- As a group, think of 3 needs that are found in your community.
- What are some ways that each of these needs could be met?

- Pick one of the needs and begin to formulate a plan for your group to meet that need.

Need: _____
We will: _____
We need help from: _____

MY ACTION:
- How can I begin to practice Christ's method of outreach everyday?

- Where in my life can I begin to ...

Mingle:
Show Sympathy:
Minister to Needs:
Win Confidence:
Invite to follow:

We naturally have needs. We can only survive a few minutes with oxygen, a few days without water, a few weeks (believe it or not) without food. We also have need for shelter, respect, health, and happiness.

While Jesus was on earth, He spent much of His time meeting the needs of others. Matthew 9:35 describes it this way, "Then Jesus went about all the cities and villages, teaching in their synagogues, preaching the gospel of the kingdom, and healing every sickness and every disease among the people."

Jesus desired to meet our "ultimate needs" ... sometimes he started with our "felt needs." What can we learn from this?

Ministry of Healing, 143 - Christ's method alone will give true success in reaching the people. The Saviour mingled with men as one who desired their good. He showed His sympathy for them, ministered to their needs, and won their confidence. Then He bade them, "Follow Me."

Launch

- What is the longest you have gone without meal? How did it feel when you could finally eat again?

- Describe the most helpful person you know. How have they been helpful to you?

Call to Action
Matt 25:34-40

Then the King will say to those on His right hand, 'Come, you blessed of My Father, inherit the kingdom prepared for you from the foundation of the world: for I was hungry and you gave Me food; I was thirsty and you gave Me drink; I was a stranger and you took Me in; I was naked and you clothed Me; I was sick and you visited Me; I was in prison and you came to Me'.... And the King will answer and say to them, 'Assuredly, I say to you, inasmuch as you did *it* to one of the least of these My brethren, you did *it* to Me.'

Felt Need - Something that is a pressing need or concern to an individual or family.
Ultimate Need - Everyone is in need of salvation through faith in Jesus.

Reflection

- Why do you think Jesus equates serving others with serving Him?

- Read the quote above. What 5 actions are included in "Christ's Method"?

- Note that the first four are about meeting people and their needs. The final action is the call to follow.

- Do you think this order is important (meet needs, then introduce to Jesus)? Why or why not?

- Often people are not ready to hear about Jesus, their ultimate need, until their felt needs have been addressed. Why do you think this is true?

- Jesus met many types of needs. Review the following stories. Fill in the blanks with the following words: Spiritual, Physical, Social, Emotional, Intellectual, Health

John 2 - Water to Wine _____ Need
John 3 - Nicodemus _____ Need
John 4 - Women at Well _____ Need
John 5 - Pool of Bethesda _____ Need
John 6 - Feeding 5000 _____ Need

APPENDIX E

SURVEY RAW DATA

Table 3

Survey Results – Averages of Answers from Year 1 and Year 2 of study

	Year 1			Year 2		
Question Summary	Pre	Post No	Post Yes	Pre	Post No	Post Yes
Pers. Spirituality	4.0	3.9	4.1	3.9	4.1	4.2
Outreach Exp.	3.2	3.1	3.4	3.2	3.3	3.2
Outreach Skills	3.1	3.0	3.5	3.1	3.0	3.2
Pray	3.3	3.2	3.3	3.3	3.2	3.3
Study Bible	3.1	2.7	3.0	3.1	3.0	3.2
Intro to Jesus	2.9	2.7	3.0	2.7	2.6	2.8
Assist in Teaching	3.2	3.1	3.7	3.0	3.1	3.3
Invite Unchurched	2.4	2.2	2.7	2.3	2.2	2.6
Praying for Others	3.6	3.3	3.7	3.4	3.2	3.5
Helping Others	3.7	3.2	3.8	3.2	3.1	3.4
Meet Small Group	2.9	2.8	3.5	2.7	2.7	3.1
Serve in Ministry	2.9	2.8	3.3	2.8	2.8	3.1
Rate Sp Health (10)	5.9	5.9	6.5	5.8	5.9	5.8
Participate in GG						
Evan Training			52%			59%
Active Outreach			33%			50%
Small Grp Interact			91%			97%
Emotional Benefit			6.2			5.0
Spiritual Benefit			6.3			5.4
Evangelism Benefit			5.1			4.6
Social Benefit			6.4			5.4

REFERENCE LIST

Adams, W. M. (2009). *Developing, planting, and multiplying an Adventist house church using principles of missiology in the Florida Conference of Seventh-day Adventists* (Doctoral dissertation). Andrews University, Seventh-day Adventist Theological Seminary, Berrien Springs, MI.

Adeney, F. (2010). *Graceful evangelism: Christian witness in a complex world.* Grand Rapids, MI: Baker Academic.

Agati, H. A. (2012). *The millennial generation: Howe and Strauss disputed* (Doctoral dissertation). Available from ProQuest Dissertations and Theses. (UMI No. 916787459)

Appleton, J. (2012). The perceptions of a missional lifestyle amongst European generation Y Christians. *Encounters Mission Journal 43*(1), 10-21. Retrieved from http://www.redcliffe.org/SpecialistCentres/EncountersMissionJournal

Barna Group. (2004, October 11). Evangelism is most effective among kids. Retrieved from https://www.barna.org/barna-update/article/5-barna-update/196-evangelism-is-most-effective-among-kids

Barna Group. (2013a, December 18). Is evangelism going out of style? Retrieved from https://www.barna.org/barna-update/faith-spirituality/648-is-evangelism-going-out-of-style

Barna Group. (2013b). *Seventh-day Adventist Church: Young adult study.* Silver Spring, MD: Seventh-day Adventist Church.

Beckworth, D., & Kidder, S. J. (2010, December). Reflections on the future of North-American Seventh-day Adventism. *Ministry Magazine, 82*(12), 20-22. Retrieved from https://www.ministrymagazine.org/archive/2010/12/reflections-on-the-future-of-north-american-seventh-day-adventism.html

Bergmann, J., & Sams, A. (2012). *Flip your classroom: Reach every student in every class every day.* Washington, DC: International Society for Technology in Education.

Black, T., & Harold, G. (2010). A New Testament approach to poverty alleviation as a social centered model for evangelism. *South African Baptist Journal of Theology, 19*(1), 74-85. Retrieved from http://www.ctbs.org.za/sa-baptist-journal-of-theology/

Bosch, D. J. (2008). Evangelism: Theological currents and cross-currents today. In P. W. Chilcote & L. C. Warner (Eds.), *The Study of evangelism: Exploring a missional practice of the church* (pp. 4-17). Grand Rapids, MI: William B. Eerdmans.

Burrill, R. (1996). *Radical disciples for revolutionary churches.* Fallbrook, CA: Hart Research Center.

Burrill, R. (1997). *The revolutionized church of the 21st century.* Fallbrook, CA: Hart Books.

Burrill, R. (2007). *Reaping the harvest.* Fallbrook, CA: Hart Books.

Burrill, R. (2009). *How to grow an Adventist church.* Fallbrook, CA: Hart Books.

Burrill, R. (2014). *Adventist evangelistic preaching.* Fallbrook, CA: Hart Books.

Carter, T. (2013). *The 4G learning community: Teaching, learning, and leading across four generations.* Bloomington, IN: Booktango.

Cole, N. (2005). *Organic church.* San Francisco, CA: Jossey-Bass.

Coleman, R. E. (1972). *The master plan of evangelism.* Terrytown, NY: Fleming H. Revell.

Cowin, T. J. (2011). *Using the small group ministry at the Rock Church of Saint Louis, Missouri, to hold Christians accountable to a missional lifestyle* (Doctoral dissertation). Retrieved from ProQuest Dissertations and Theses (UMI No. 909969375).

Creps, E. (2008). *Reverse mentoring: How young leaders can transform the church and why we should let them.* San Francisco, CA: Jossey-Bass.

Crocker, D. (2008). *The Samaritan way: Lifestyle compassion ministry.* St. Louis, MO: Chalice Press.

Dean, K. C. (2010). *Almost Christian: What the faith of our teenagers is telling the American church.* New York, NY: Oxford University Press.

Decker, M. (2007). The emerging college generation and missions: Issues, attitudes, postures and passions. *Evangelical Missions Quarterly, 43*(3), 316-323.

DeVries, M. (2008). *Sustainable youth ministry: Why most youth ministry doesn't last and what your church can do about it.* Downers Grove, IL: InterVarsity.

Drane, J. (2008). *After McDonaldization: Mission, ministry, and Christian discipleship in an age of uncertainty.* Grand Rapids, MI: Zondervan.

Easum, W. M., & Atkinson, J. (2007). *Go big with small groups: Eleven steps to an explosive small group ministry.* Nashville, TN: Abingdon.

Elmore, T. (2010). *Generation iY: Our last chance to save their future.* Atlanta, GA: Poet Gardener.

Elmore, T. (2013). *Managing the toughest generation* [ebook]. Retrieved from http://growingleaders.com/Leadership-Training-Young-Professionals

Engelmann, K. V. (2010). *Soul-shaping small groups: A refreshing approach for exasperated leaders.* Downers Grove, IL: InterVarsity.

Ferguson, D., & Ferguson, J. (2010). *Exponential.* Grand Rapids, MI: Zondervan.

Garland, D. R., & Edmonds, J. A. (2007). Family life of Baptists. *Family and Community Ministries: Empowering Through Faith, 21*(1), 6-21. Retrieved from http://www.baylor.edu/fcm_journal/

Gehring, R. W. (2004). *House church and mission: The importance of household structures in early Christianity.* Peabody, MA: Hendrickson.

Georgia-Cumberland Academy. (2016). School history [website]. Retrieved from http://gcasda.org/about/school-history

Georgia-Cumberland Academy Church. (2016a). *Church membership statistical report.* Calhoun, GA: Author.

Georgia-Cumberland Academy Church. (2016b). Discipleship plan [website]. Retrieved from gcachurch.org/discipleship-plan

Gladen, S. (2011). *Small groups with purpose: How to create healthy communities.* Grand Rapids, MI: Baker Books.

Gortner, D. (2008). *Transforming evangelism.* New York, NY: Church Publishing.

Halter, H., & Smay, M. (2010). *And: The gathered and scattered church.* Grand Rapids, MI: Zondervan.

Hill, G. (2012). *Salt, light, and a city: Introducing missional ecclesiology.* Eugene, OR: Wipf & Stock.

House, B. (2011). *Community: Taking your small group off life support.* Wheaton, IL: Crossway.

Howe, N., & Nadler, R. (2010). *Millennials in the workplace.* Great Falls, VA: LifeCourse Associates.

Howe, N., & Strauss, W. (2000). *Millennials rising: The next great generation.* New York, NY: Vintage.

Hudson, G. (Producer). (2016). *EquipPodcast: For total member involvement.* [Audio Podcast]. Retrieved from http://equippodcast.wordpress.com

James, D. (2005). *Orientation to holistic small groups and the journey of discipleship.* Berrien Springs, MI: Open Home Ministries.

Jeffers, J. S. (1999). *The Greco-Roman world of the New Testament era: Exploring the background of early Christianity.* Downers Grove, IL: InterVarsity Press.

Johnson, K. W. (2011). *Successful small groups: From theory to reality.* Hagerstown, MD: Review and Herald.

Jones, R. P., Cox, D. C., & Banchoff, T. (2012). *A generation in transition: Religion, values, and politics among college-age Millennials – findings from the 2012 Millennial values survey.* Retrieved from http://berkleycenter.georgetown.edu/ millennialvaluessurvey

Keller, T. (1989). *Ministries of mercy: The call of the Jericho road.* Phillipsburg, NJ: P & R Pub.

Keller, T. (2012). *Center church: Doing balanced, gospel-centered ministry in your city.* Grand Rapids, MI: Zondervan.

Kidder, J. (2011). *The big four: Secrets to a thriving church family.* Hagerstown, MD: Review and Herald.

Kimball, D. (2007). *They like Jesus but not the church.* Grand Rapids, MI: Zondervan.

Kinnaman, D., & Hawkins, A. (2011). *You lost me: Why young Christians are leaving church, and rethinking faith.* Grand Rapids, MI: Baker Books.

Kirk, J. A., Anderson, J., Crockett, M., Lucey-Lee, U., McWilliams, J., Teng, T., & Van Opstal, S. (2009). *Small group leaders' handbook: Developing transformational communities.* Downers Grove, IL: InterVarsity.

Kranz, J. (2014, March 9). All the 'one another' commands in the NT [Web blog post]. Retrieved from http://overviewbible.com/one-another-infographic/

Latini, T. F. (2011). *The church and the crisis of community: A practical theology of small-group ministry.* Grand Rapids, MI: William B. Eerdmans.

Leonard, B. J. (2008). Evangelism and contemporary American life. In P. W. Chilcote & L. C. Warner (Eds.), *The Study of evangelism: Exploring a missional practice of the church*. Grand Rapids, MI: William B. Eerdmans.

Mason, M., Singleton, A., & Webber, R. (2007). *The spirit of Generation Y: Young people's spirituality in a changing Australia*. Mulgrave, Victoria, Australia: John Garratt.

McKey, D. (2016, August 5). Essential keys to total member involvement. *Review and Herald* [Online article]. Retrieved from http://www.adventistreview.org/church-news/story4227-essential-keys-to-total-member-involvement.

McNeal, R. (2009). *Missional renaissance: Changing the scorecard for the church*. San Francisco, CA: Jossey-Bass.

McNeal, R. (2013). *Get off your donkey! Help somebody and help yourself*. Grand Rapids, MI: Baker Books.

Morris, D. (2009). *The radical teachings of Jesus*. Hagerstown, MD: Review and Herald.

Morris, D. (2015, November 5). The media revolution and youth ministry [Web log post]. Retrieved from www.ministrymagazine.org/blog/2015/11/05/the-media-revolution-and-youth-ministry

Nichol, F. D. (1953). *The Seventh-day Adventist Bible commentary: The Holy Bible with exegetical and expository comment* (Vol. 6). Washington, DC: Review and Herald.

North American Division of Seventh-day Adventists. (2014). *Building Together*. Retrieved from http://www.adventistchurchconnect.com/site/1/docs/Transformational_Evangelism.pdf

O'Malley, A. L., & Williams, D. E. (2012). Emerging leaders: The roles of flourishing and religiosity in Millennials' leadership development activity. *Journal of Spirituality, Leadership and Management, 6*(1), 48-58. Retrieved from http://www.slam.org.au/publications/journal/

Office of Archives, Statistics, and Research, General Conference of Seventh-day Adventists. (2015). Georgia-Cumberland Conference (1932-Present). In *Adventist Statistics*. Retrieved December 8, 2015 from http://www.adventiststatistics.org/view_Summary.asp?FieldID=C10169#SubFields

Pauline, J. (2008). *Everlasting gospel, ever-changing world: Introducing Jesus to a skeptical generation*. Nampa, ID: Pacific Press.

Petty, K. (2007). *Externally focused small groups: How churches are re-engineering their small groups for community service.* Leadership Network. Retrieved from http://www.navigators.ca/SGN/pdf/ExternallyFocusedSmallGroups.pdf

Portnoy, G., & Wurzback, C. (1982). Theme from "cheers" (where everyboy knows your name). [single]. Los Angeles, CA: Paramount.

Powell, K., & Clark, C. (2011). *Sticky faith: Everyday ideas to build lasting faith in your kids.* Grand Rapids, MI: Zondervan.

Powell, K., Mulder, J., & Griffin, B. (2016). *Growing young: Six essential strategies to helping young people discover and live your church.* Grand Rapids, MI: Baker Books.

Putnam, D. (2008). *Breaking the discipleship code.* Nashville, TN: B & H Pub.

Rainer, T. S., & Geiger, E. (2006). *Simple church: Returning to God's process for making disciples.* Nashville, TN: Broadman Press.

Rainer, T. S., & Rainer, J. W. (2011). *The Millennials: Connecting to America's largest generation.* Nashville, TN: B & H Pub.

Rideout, V. (2015). *The common sense census: Media use by tweens and teens.* San Francisco, CA: Common Sense Media.

Roxburgh, A. (2011). *Missional: Joining God in the neighborhood.* Grand Rapids, MI: Baker Books.

Roxburgh, A., & Boren, M. S. (2009*). Introducing the missional church: What it is, why it matters, how to become one.* Grand Rapids, MI: Baker Books.

Sahlin, M, (2004). *Understanding your community.* Lincoln, NB: Center for Creative Ministry.

Sahlin, M. (2007). *Mission in metropolis: The Adventist movement in an urban world.* Lincoln, NE: Center for Creative Ministry.

Searcy, N. (2008). *Activate: An entirely new approach to small groups.* Ventura, CA: Regal.

Searcy, N., & Henson, J. (2009). *Ignite.* Grand Rapids, MI: Baker.

Seemiller, C., & Grace, M. (2016). Generation z goes to college. San Francisco, CA: Jossey-Bass.

Serns, D. (2015). *Army of youth* [website]. Retrieved from https://danserns .wordpress.com/texas-evangelism-beta/your-congregation/army-of-youth/

Sherr, M., Garland, D., & Wolfer, T. (2007). The role of community service in the faith development of adolescents. *Journal of Youth Ministry, 6*(1), 43-54.

Sider, R. J. (1997). *Rich Christians in an age of hunger: Moving from affluence to generosity.* Dallas, TX: Word.

Sjogren, S. (2003). *Conspiracy of kindness: A unique approach to sharing the love of Jesus* (2nd ed.). Ventura, CA: Regal.

Smith, C., & Denton, M. L. (2005). *Soul searching: The religious and spiritual lives of American teenagers.* New York, NY: Oxford University Press.

Smith, C., & Snell, P. (2009). *Souls in transition: The religious and spiritual lives of emerging adults.* New York, NY: Oxford University Press.

Smith, K. (2010). *The effects of service-learning on Millennial students* (Doctoral dissertation). Retrieved from ProQuest Dissertations and Theses. (UMI No. 3438782)

Stallard, M. (2011). Gospel centeredness, Jesus, and social ethics. *The Journal of Ministry and Theology, 15*(2), 5-24. Retrieved from http://www.galaxie.com/article/jmat15-2-01

Stanley, A., & Willits, B. (2004). *Creating community: Five keys to building a small group culture.* Sisters, OR: Multnomah.

Stetzer, E., & Geiger, E. (2014). *Transformational groups: Creating a new scorecard for groups.* Nashville, TN: B & H.

Stetzer, E., & Putnam, D. (2006). *Breaking the missional code.* Nashville, TN: Broadman & Holman.

Stetzer, E., & Rainer, T. S. (2010). *Transformational church: Creating a new scorecard for congregations.* Nashville, TN: B & H.

Stetzer, E., Stanley, R., & Hayes, J. (2009). *Lost and found: The younger unchurched and the churches that reach them.* Nashville, TN: B & H.

Swanson, E., & Rusaw, R. (2010). *The externally focused quest: Becoming the best church for the community.* San Francisco, CA: Jossey-Bass.

Sweet, L. (1999). *SoulTsunami.* Grand Rapids, MI: Zondervan.

Thayer, J. (1999). *The Christian spiritual participation profile.* Author.

Thayer, O. J. (2004). Constructing a spirituality measure based on learning theory: The Christian spiritual participation profile. *Journal of Psychology and Christianity 23*(3), 195-207.

Trim, D. (2016). Data on youth retention and connectedness to the church. Office of Archives, Statistics, and Research, General Conference of Seventh-day Adventists. Retrieved from http://www.adventistresearch .org/sites/default/files/files/Annual%20Council%202016%20Presentation%20on %20Youth%20Retention%2C%20David%20Trim.pdf

Warren, R. (1995). *The purpose driven church: Growth without compromising your message and mission.* Grand Rapids, MI: Zondervan.

Wheeler, D. (2009). *Together in prayer: Coming to God in community.* Downers Grove, IL: InterVarsity Press.

White, E. G. (1902). *Testimonies for the church* (Vol. 7). Mountain View, CA: Pacific Press.

White, E. G. (1903). *Education.* Mountain View, CA: Pacific Press.

White, E. G. (1905). *The ministry of healing.* Mountain View, CA: Pacific Press.

White, E. G. (1911). *The acts of the apostles.* Mountain View, CA: Pacific Press.

White, E. G. (1915). *Gospel workers.* Washington, DC: Review and Herald.

White, E. G. (1946). *Evangelism.* Washington, DC: Review and Herald.

White, J. E. (2014). *The rise of the nones.* Grand Rapids, MI: Baker Books.

Whitehead, R., & Boyd, J. (2008). Church of refuge: A support ministry for youth and young adults [website]. Retrieved from http://www.cye.org/article/118/cye-ministries/church-of-refuge/resources

Winograd, M., & Hais, M. (2011). *Millennial momentum: How a new generation is remaking America.* New Brunswick, NJ: Rutgers University Press.

We invite you to view the complete
selection of titles we publish at:
www.TEACHServices.com

We encourage you to write us
with your thoughts about this,
or any other book we publish at:
info@TEACHServices.com

TEACH Services' titles may be purchased in
bulk quantities for educational, fund-raising,
business, or promotional use.
bulksales@TEACHServices.com

Finally, if you are interested in seeing
your own book in print, please contact us at:
publishing@TEACHServices.com

We are happy to review your manuscript at no charge.

www.ingramcontent.com/pod-product-compliance
Lightning Source LLC
Chambersburg PA
CBHW080603170426
43196CB00017B/2891